INSIDE THE WALLS OF MY OWN HOUSE: THE COMPLETE *DARK SHADOWS* (OF MY CHILDHOOD)

BOOK 2

D1519208

INSIDE THE WALLS OF MY OWN HOUSE: THE COMPLETE *DARK SHADOWS* (OF MY CHILDHOOD)

BOOK 2

TONY TRIGILIO

BLAZEVOX[BOOKS]
Buffalo, New York

publisher of weird little books

BlazeVOX [books]

blazevox.org

BlazeVOX

FOR LIZ

A TV program produced for adults is viewed by a small child. Half of what is said and done in the TV drama is probably misunderstood by the child. Maybe it's all *misunderstood. And the thing is, just how authentic is the information anyhow, even if the child correctly understood it?*

—Philip K. Dick,
"How to Build a Universe That Doesn't
Fall Apart Two Days Later"

Table of Contents

INSIDE THE WALLS OF MY OWN HOUSE:
THE COMPLETE *DARK SHADOWS*
(OF MY CHILDHOOD)

BOOK 2

Behind the Scenes: My Barnabas Collins

Dark Shadows was a soap opera broadcast weekdays on the ABC television network from 1966-1971. The show set itself apart from other daytime soaps with its relentlessly gothic aesthetic and plotlines built around ghosts and other supernatural phenomena. The uncanny became a permanent feature of *Dark Shadows*. It remains the only haunted soap opera in American TV history.

On April 17, 1967 (Episode 210), the show introduced the character of Barnabas Collins, a vampire from the eighteenth century accidentally freed from his chained coffin in 1967 by a grave robber, Willie Loomis. The show's producers originally intended to keep the Barnabas character around for only a 13-week narrative arc. But he quickly became the most popular character on the show, and he remained a central figure from April 1967 through the show's cancellation in 1971.

Barnabas Collins was the star of nearly all my childhood nightmares. I watched the show every day with my mother, a devoted soap opera fan, in the first months and years of my life—and many of my earliest memories are terrifying recollections of Barnabas stalking me. I was petrified by Barnabas; at the same time, the vampire also was an object of insatiable curiosity for me. My feelings about Barnabas were nurtured and sustained before I came into language, and are twined with some of my most primal sensations.

Production Notes

This is the second book of a multivolume poem. I intend to watch all 1,225 episodes of *Dark Shadows*, composing one sentence for each episode and shaping each sentence into verse form. Book 1 began with Episode 210 (Barnabas rising from the dead) and ended with Episode 392. Book 2 resumes with Episode 393 and continues through Episode 573. As in Book 1, the epigraphs at the beginning of each section are taken from the *Dark Shadows* introductory teasers spoken by individual characters in voice-over at the beginning of each episode.

I will return to Episodes 1-209 in the final volume, as a kind of prequel/coda, after I have watched the last episode of the series. The show was preempted 20 times during its five-year run, and in these instances the network double-numbered or triple-numbered the episodes so that the show airing on a Friday would always end in a 5 or a 0. The final episode of *Dark Shadows*, then, is officially Episode 1,245, even though it was actually the 1,225th episode produced for the show.

The author wishes to thank the editors of the following journals in which excerpts appeared, often in different versions: *Court Green*, *Cream City Review*, *Goreyesque*, and *TriQuarterly*. Thanks to Ellipsis Coffeehouse for providing a terrific environment to work on this book (and for some of the best coffee in Chicago). Warm, undead gratitude to Jan Bottiglieri, Brian Cremins, Matthew DeMarco, Allison Felus, Geoffrey Gatza, Chris Green, Liz Shulman, Michael Trigilio, and David Trinidad.

Previously in The Complete Dark Shadows (of My Childhood), Book 1

I began Book 1 on May 31, 2011, watching Episode 210 of *Dark Shadows* (originally broadcast April 17, 1967). I composed my first response to the show as two-bit thug Willie Loomis freed 207-year-old vampire Barnabas Collins from his chained coffin inside a secret tomb in the small New England seaport town of Collinsport, Maine. Released from his casket, Barnabas immediately became the bloodsucking mystery scourge of Collinsport.

Jonathan Frid, the actor who played Barnabas, died in the book's tenth month. I received news of Frid's death the day after my limited-edition, coffin-shaped *Dark Shadows* DVD collection arrived—the boxed set titled *"Dark Shadows": The Complete Original Series*, which I later adapted for the title of this project—and I commemorated, in rhyming couplets, Frid's passing into spirit. Barely 30 pages into the book, I already had outlived the star of my childhood nightmares. But I was afraid to write that I'd "outlived" Frid—scared I might be smugly tempting the universe to hasten my own demise. I'd survived Frid, but could I live long enough to write 1,225 sentences in response to 1,225 episodes? This would not be the last time that the sheer scope of this project induced fears of my own mortality. As I fell deeper into Book 1, the project began to reveal itself more clearly: this was a long poem less indebted to the "anxiety of influence" as it was to the influence of anxiety.

A couple months later, almost a full year after I began the project, I survived Tim Burton's 2012 remake of *Dark Shadows*, in which Johnny Depp turned the sadistic vampire scourge of my childhood nightmares into a camp buffoon. I continued to watch and write one sentence per episode, shaping memoiristic recollection into verse while excavating my childhood vampire nightmares (and the firm persuasion they produced in me, as a toddler, that I could protect myself from being bitten on the neck if I hunched my shoulders before going to sleep at night).

I juggled other poetry and editorial projects while writing Book I, and my work on these manuscripts took me from my home, Chicago, to California, New Hampshire, France, and the Netherlands, among other locales, as part of what became the book's extended travelogue sequences. I chronicled all of my trips—including a fruitless search for Apollinaire's grave with my wife Liz in Paris—in what was soon becoming a gigantic, sprawling, ekphrastic diary poem in which my viewing of *Dark Shadows* asserted itself as an insistent presence, day after day, in my life with Liz, our cats, our friends, and our families.

The project was becoming more consciously an experiment in autobiography, documenting my life as I watched (and documented) episode after episode of *Dark Shadows*. Still, with over a thousand episodes to watch and over a thousand sentences to write, I feared the poem was becoming an impossible object. I continued to worry that I would need at least a couple decades to view all 1,225 episodes of the show and, in response, write 1,225 sentences and shape them into a long poem. Book I reflects my ongoing anxiety that I am creating an ersatz epic whose grandiose scope reflects nothing more than an experiment in neurotic fanaticism, like Ken Applegate's *Matchstick Space Shuttle*—a spaceship replica that required 10 years of design, 12 years of construction, and one million wooden matchsticks—which I first saw, during the early stages of Book I, at the San Francisco Ripley's Believe It or Not! museum.

But then again, I love the *Matchstick Space Shuttle*, and I hope Book I conveys my reverence for the single-pointed fixation required to conceive, execute, and actually finish that kind of project. In this way, the poem never stops being an exploration of obsession. The poem's form and content followed me (haunted me?) everywhere I went as I wrote Book I. Whether trundling through outsider art at the Ripley's museum, sitting in a library in New Hampshire doing research for other poems, or visiting friends in Paris, I found it impossible *not* to continue building my impossible object of a poem.

In late autumn 2012—or 1967 in the world of the show—*Dark Shadows* meandered into a 1795 plotline that continued for the book's final 28 sentences (i.e., episodes). A 1967 séance held in the Great House of Collinwood tore a supernatural rip in the daytime soap opera time-space continuum, and the show's characters assumed the roles of their eighteenth-century doppelgängers as *Dark Shadows* explored the origin story of Barnabas, the vampire. Book 1 ended the way it began, with actor Tim Gordon's arm rising from the grave, opening and closing itself in a choke hold. Characters still couldn't stay buried. Barnabas still was a threat to Collinsport (and to sensitive, insomniac children watching with their mothers at home). Actors still flubbed their lines. Stagehands could still be heard coughing offstage. Shadows of boom mics still cast themselves on soundstage walls. I still watched and wrote.

INSIDE THE WALLS OF MY OWN HOUSE: THE COMPLETE *DARK SHADOWS* (OF MY CHILDHOOD)

BOOK 2

I.

A séance has been held in the Great House at Collinwood—a séance which has suspended time and space and sent one woman on an uncertain and frightening journey into the past, back to the year 1795.

And Book 2 begins: I'm still stuck
in 1795, watching *Dark Shadows*

tonight in Boston, a hotel two miles
from my old apartment in the Fenway.

I'm attending a conference with 12,000
other writers—I'd be happier alone

writing—forced this week into the jostle
and clot of full-house readings

at cafés and bars all over Boston,
where, in 1995, living in my small

one-bedroom at 40 Queensberry St.,
I composed an unfinished essay

(single-spaced, dot-matrix, on flimsy
compost-brown recyclable paper)

in which I tried to make grown-up
sense of the Barnabas night terrors

of my childhood: *I watched "Dark
Shadows" with my mother every day,*

I wrote, *looking for secret messages
meant for me alone—Barnabas seething*

for my blood; the essay stops on page two,
after I confess my childhood belief

Barnabas actually lived inside the walls
of our home like some kind of vampire

termite; Barnabas watching from
inside the inside of our house—

how else could he get into my head
so easily every night when I slept

(no surprise I nearly failed my first
logic class in college, weaned on hard-

headed realists like Josette's father, André,
who finds torn, bloody sheets strewn

around the shamble of Jeremiah's
bedroom in the Great House and says,

"I find it difficult to believe something
supernatural could have caused all this,

but what other answer is there?").

————————————

As a wedding gift, Naomi deeds
the Old House to Barnabas and his

witch-bride, Angelique, whose saucy,
spectral grin threatens to pull apart

her face—and the camera backs off,
making a drunken, hairpin turn from

Naomi's pinched lips to a blurred close-up
of her puffy black blouse and ruffled collar.

Happy New Year, 1968: the Tet Offensive
starts all over South Vietnam in 29 days

and Jeremiah is now played in death—
fatally shot in his dual with Barnabas

—by Tim Gordon, a *Dark Shadows* extra
whose hand was used for the famous

shot in Episode 210 of the vampire
reaching from his casket to choke

grave-robbing Willie Loomis; a ghost,
his head wrapped in bloody bandages,

Gordon takes over the part from
Anthony George, who was Jeremiah

after playing Burke Devlin in 1967
(replacing the show's first Burke,

Mitch Ryan, who was fired for
showing up drunk to rehearsals

and tapings): Jeremiah's ghost takes
revenge on Angelique, burying her

alive, inaugurating the first day of
the second year of my life with another

of director Lela Swift's familiar first-
person POV interment shots, Jeremiah

looking down on us (my mother
and I watching on New Year's Day,

seeing everything through the eyes
of Angelique lying in Jeremiah's

open grave), the ghost dropping
handfuls of dirt on the camera lens,

leaving viewers with persistent
afterimages of being buried alive,

the soil slowly covering them whole.

———————————————

In Pittsburgh, after a reading organized
by Jan Beatty and Kayla Sargeson,

watching the show in my hotel room,
the Shadyside Inn (packed my DVD drive

and a box of *Dark Shadows* discs, as I do
every trip): don't expect me to believe

the minister chosen to marry Barnabas,
a vampire-in-waiting, and Angelique, a witch

buried alive, is actually named "Rev. Bland."

———————————————

Love, American-style: Angelique suffers
insomnia on their wedding night, Barnabas

misses cues and stumbles over his lines.

———————————————

Just in case we forgot the end of yesterday's
episode, Angelique talks to herself, narrating

the entire final scene—Ben Stokes
caught stealing a black hair ribbon

from Abigail Collins's bedroom—
the witch-bride's maniacal reflection

glowing in an Old House mirror;
Angelique's voice-over speaks right

back to her, garbled and distorted
like a desperate ham radio transmission.

Rev. Trask celebrates Episode 400 with
another clumsy exorcism—this time using

a dowsing rod whose tips he set on fire
(how often I followed the smoke that rose

in double helixes from my mother's Salems,
transfixed, watching her watch *Dark Shadows*,

vapors wending their way to the ceiling).

———————————————

Poor sap: Ben Stokes escapes the Collins
family dungeon in the Old House

basement—where Barnabas will imprison
Maggie Evans in 1967—only to find

himself trapped in the prison-house
of language: "I know who the witch is,"

he says, "but I can't write her name."

———————————————

"'A' is for Angelique," Barnabas says after
Ben scratches the witch's initial in dust

(Cold comfort for the vampire-in-waiting).
Don't listen to Barnabas, Countess du Prés:

Everyone you've met in the haunted Collins
Family is enchanted by visions, wisps,

Ghosts, exorcists (and now a 1967 bat prop
Hovering above Barnabas and Josette).

I admit I'm growing fond of 1795:
Josette, puzzled, studies the chroma-

Keyed, time-traveling bat, its fox face
Leering back at her vintage art-school

Mourning dress; a fake bat—Little David's
Nemesis, last seen flitting about Episode 341—

Ominous red eyes and distorted, low-fi
Prerecorded chirping: the prop's bloodstruck

Quiver as it dangles from a stagehand's string.
Rainy April night in Chicago, and Angelique

Slings her dying hex, *finally*, upon Barnabas;
Taking one last breath, the spurned witch-bride

Utters a spell that brings back the chirpy
Vampire bat (the shabby little prop

Wobbles when it bites Barnabas's neck),
Explaining, after 40 episodes of 18th-century

Yackety-yacking, how Barnabas Collins got
Zapped for eternity by a vampire curse:

"A" is for Angelique—and abecedarian fatigue!

———————————————

"I'd like to see Barnabas turn into
a vampire," Liz texted from New York,

where she presented a paper at a post-
colonial conference (the essay she wrote

last summer with Tal in Paris, when Ghost
Girl and Little David, the psychic child,

scampered around the cemetery, trying
to figure out who's dead and who isn't):

I needed *Dark Shadows* to escape CNN's
constant video loop of the Boston Marathon

bombing, bloody sidewalks in Copley Sq.,
where I used to catch the Queensberry St.

bus every day, the discordant violin/theremin
clash at Barnabas's bedside ("Mistah Barnabas

needs the care of a doctor, not a witch,"
Ben Stokes says, in his scratchy Maine

brogue, to Angelique, who's not quite
dead yet) blocking out the sounds

of two bombs exploding 210 yards
from each other 12 seconds apart;

almost every year I walked there,
after the runners finished and crowds

cleared, often the first long, aimless stroll
of spring; trundling through the debris,

countless water bottles and paper cups,
I could feel my city jolt awake, spring

arriving each year covered in Boylston St.
litter (I'm watching *Dark Shadows* tonight

to avoid looking at the blood stains).

———————————

Kübler-Ross's five stages of vampirism:
one, fever delirium—hearing your mother's

botched lines spoken in underwater reverb;
two, blurred vision; three, your witch-bride

throws open the curtains and you
shriek at the daylight coming through

the window; four, you're suddenly
compelled to wear a psychedelic,

Pre-Raphaelite smoking jacket;
five, the bat-bite puncture wounds

on your neck won't stop bleeding
and your undead eye shadow

thickens with each new scene.

_____

To commemorate my 200th episode,
and celebrate the arrival of the first

proofs for Book 1 of *The Complete
Dark Shadows (of My Childhood)*,

emailed by Geoffrey Gatza this morning,
I went to eBay and bought a copy

of the Episode 1 script, which I
actually can't write about until

I reach this poem's prequel/coda
sometime in the next decade

(confession: I cheated last summer
and drafted Episode 1's sentence—

I couldn't resist the DVD extra
included in the coffin's first disc:

the 6/27/66 original broadcast, with
commercials, of the first episode):

"When you said, '200th episode,'
I thought about the 20 years I spent

watching *All My Children*," Liz says,
as Barnabas tosses and turns in his

deathbed, tortured by memories of
the time-traveling bat prop from 1967

whose fatal bite is turning him into
a vampire, "which comes out to about

250 episodes a year, when you account
for holidays and preemptions"—

roughly 5,000 episodes of *All My Children*,
the entire *Dark Shadows* oeuvre multiplied

by four; later, Liz and I watch Barnabas die:
surely, my childhood tormentor's demise

was a narcotic balm for me in 1968
(until I went to bed that night and my

Dark Shadows nightmares resumed).
First sundown after Barnabas's death:

"If he comes to life, he'll settle *you!*"
Ben Stokes says to the witch Angelique,

trapping her, with Barnabas's coffin,
in the secret chamber of the Collins

family mausoleum, after the word
"vampire" is uttered for the first time

on *Dark Shadows*—of course, another
episode directed by Lela Swift, whose

fetish for sealing characters in coffins
and mausoleums fed an early phobia,

to be buried alive, a fear that made me
afraid to go to sleep in 1972, age six,

when I saw *The Longest Night*, starring
David Janssen and James Farentino,

an ABC Movie of the Week based on
the true story of young real estate heiress

Barbara Jane Mackle, kidnapped in 1968
and imprisoned in a coffin underground

(her captors sealed her in the casket with
a battery-powered air pump and gallon

of sedative-laced water, enough to survive
for a few days, waiting for her parents

to pay the half-million-dollar ransom).

———————————————

Song of myself, hunching my shoulders
in bed to prevent Barnabas from biting

my neck in the middle of the night:
stop this day with me and you will

possess the origin of all poems
about my vampire nightmares—

you shall no longer take things at second
or third hand—you will look through

the eyes of the dead, feed on the spectres
in books: Barnabas's ruffle-sleeved hand

rises from his casket and chokes to death
the witch Angelique before she can drive

a holly-tree stake through his vampire heart.

———————————

"The ways of a witch are not necessarily
determined by reason and understanding,"

Rev. Trask says, wagging his finger outside
Victoria's cell in the Collinsport Gaol.

Let me get this straight, Victoria: you think
if you correctly predict Sarah Collins's future,

then Naomi, Sarah's mother, will somehow
believe you're *not* a witch (death from

pneumonia for Sarah, who will return
to Collinwood in 1967 as Ghost Girl,

and her gravestone will read "1786-1796,"
even though she's going to die in 1795);

no time to think about Victoria's witchy
prophecy—an inexplicable 15-second

close-up of a stock-photo sunset intrudes,
followed by 17 seconds fixed on two more

twilight photographs, accompanied by 11 tolls
of a church bell and a shuffling stagehand's

shoes picked up by a live microphone.

———————————

In Milwaukee, after a pilgrimage
to Woodland Pattern Book Center—

our weekend by water, picking up
Wave Books's new archival edition

of Lorine Niedecker's *Lake Superior*
and her *Homemade Poems*, just released

in the CUNY Center for the Humanities
"Lost & Found" series—Navy Lieutenant

Nathan Forbes and Millicent Collins
lose track of Sarah while watching

an eclipse, and Barnabas struggles
with his urge to drain a prostitute's

blood at the waterfront (he lunges,
she falls off the dock and drowns).

Sarah, in bed, mute with pneumonia:
she's never been happier—she didn't

have to memorize any lines; I'll miss her
awkward Baltimore/cockney patois

("If only other people had the humanity
Barnabas does as a vampire," Liz says,

as Sarah dies in her undead brother's arms).

———————————————

"A little bird flew to the window,"
Naomi says, after quaffing another

glass of sherry, "it hovered there
for a moment and then flew away."

Barnabas just wants to look at Josette
one last time, stare at her while she's

sleeping; apparently, I was an object
of the same curiosity: perched outside

my bedroom window night after night,
the vampire watched me squirm until

I found a position comfortable enough
to sleep with my shoulders hunched.

"It was the wind in the woods,
Miss Josette," Ben Stokes says—

no, it was the needy, plaintive
voice of Josette's undead fiancé,

still ashamed of his vampirism,
stumbling around the cemetery

like a child lost in a department store.

———————————————

Trapped in 1795 with 21st-century
expectations for narrative logic:

I can't be the only viewer who notices
Josette isn't even remotely curious how

Barnabas returned from the dead;
star-crossed lovers with a taste for goth

reunited in the Collins family mausoleum,
the vampire's eye shadow smudged in

dim moonlight through the window
(I've seen the inside of the Collins

tomb so often that the three caskets
before the secret room are just pieces

of furniture—morbid footlockers);
later, a new character appears in

Collinsport: Navy Lt. Nathan Forbes's
jilted wife, who traveled all the way

from Baltimore, arriving the same night
Nathan finally chose a wedding date

for himself and Millicent Collins—a month
from now, in time for spring's first thaw,

according to the *Farmers' Almanac*
(he's actually holding an edition

of *The Old Farmer's Almanac*, featuring
quaint colonial zodiac images of seed-time

and harvest on the cover, a design
the publication didn't adopt until

1851, a half century after Nathan
consulted it)—and she's called Suki,

a name I'll spell "Sookie" in homage to
Sookie Stackhouse, *True Blood's* restless

human-faerie hybrid and vampire mistress.

———————————————

Welcome to haunted Collinsport,
Sookie: yes, that *was* a man lurking

at the window wearing an Inverness
cape and hiding behind garish eye

shadow; when I was a boy, trying
to sleep without exposing my bare

neck, he studied me through my street-
facing bedroom window, quizzical

and predatory ("If Barnabas were here,"
Millicent asks, flouncing around the Great

House drawing room like a vaudeville
marionette, "why would he be standing

in the woods in the dead of night?").

———————————

Fifty-seven episodes (and counting)
trapped in 1795: "Every day here

is a series of prepared speeches,"
Countess du Prés says to Josette,

who can't stop touching her own
neck—two fang wounds throbbing.

Barnabas steps through a secret panel
in the wall of Josette's bedroom: proof

for me in 1968 that a vampire lived
inside the walls of my own house;

no matter how rationally my mother
explained that no living or undead

creatures could exist inside the inside of
our home, *Dark Shadows* made me believe

in a world of paranormal certainty
(as did her books on the Salem witch

trials); my natural supernaturalism
diminished slightly as I got older,

overwhelmed by the insistent claims
of reason, the same dull round of everything

we already know: my childhood city,
Erie, Pennsylvania, was a state of mind,

a malaise, a place where homes
did not come with secret panels,

all the factories were shutting down,
welfare milk and cheese supplemented

our weekly groceries, and we swam
in a polluted Great Lake barely safer

than the fetid country ponds on the outskirts
of the city; to this day, I still feel a little dirty

when I go out to dinner with friends
(my family couldn't afford to dine out,

though my first job was in a restaurant,
age 16; my boss, nicknamed Zorba,

later convicted with his brother, Larry,
of trying to kill Larry's wife, Josie,

with the knife he showed off during
slow periods in the kitchen; when Zorba

attacked her, Josie ducked and was scalped
—her testimony sent them to prison):

if you grow up poor, you assume everyone
is watching for the inevitable moment

that reveals you're a fraud—I expect
my fellow diners are waiting for me

to paw the food into my mouth with dirty
hands, slop it down in grunts and belches;

no surprise Erie's on my mind, the decrepit
rust-belt city of my childhood, long undead

before I was even born: I inaugurated
this summer (June now in Chicago,

metallic fish odor of a different Great Lake
clinging to my T-shirt every time I come

back from jogging) with a trashy true-crime
tome, *Pizza Bomber: The Untold Story of America's*

Most Shocking Bank Robbery—any book
that sneaks the phrase "The Untold Story"

into its subtitle is pure candy—the tale
of Brian Wells, doomed Erie pizza delivery

driver who robbed a bank with a bomb
strapped to his neck and was blown up

before the bomb squad could rescue him
(bonus movie trivia: Erie provided several

location shots for the film adaptation
of Cormac McCarthy's post-apocalyptic

novel *The Road*—my squalid hometown
representing for audiences worldwide

what the end of civilization looks like).

"Why are you at Collinwood, pretending
to be someone you are not?" asks Barnabas,

whose parents are pretending he sailed
to England, a lie they tell Collinsport to hide

that he died of the plague (which they
don't know was actually a vampire curse),

right before he strangles Sookie to death
—she discovered he really doesn't live

on the other side of the ocean
and he can turn into a bat at will.

I can't tell from Naomi's hurried, curt
episode introduction whether she's angered

or bored by Sookie's death: "The evil
which plagues the family," Naomi says

of the extended Collins brood, "makes itself
seen and felt in many ways, one of which

will be death by violent means" (Sookie lived
in Collinsport just five episodes; all my plans

for future Sookie Stackhouse references
dashed for now, I apologize for dangling

True Blood allusions like a fake bat prop
from a stagehand's string and then taking

them away from the poem altogether).

———————————————

"Does Countess du Prés's reaction shot
look like an orgasm shudder or a stomach

cramp?" I asked Liz the day we spent
four hours sitting at Dolores Park

in San Francisco, where I wrote down
everything I saw in the park on a blank

page in back of *Ten Thousand Things to Do*,
Jesse Reklaw's diary comic, a collection

of four-panel autobiographical strips
he drew every day from 9/17/08

to 9/16/09 (obviously a kindred spirit,
and I plan to introduce myself to him

by email when I'm done with his book):
the cityscape with Transamerica Pyramid

clumped on the horizon between two
palm trees; bumblebees; dragonflies;

honeybees; a small yapping dog;
lazy sunbathers; the Muni bus gliding

down its cable on Church Street;
a wedding party spread on a blanket

at the bottom of our hill (a woman
pulled out an acoustic guitar, then

they cut the cake); kids on swings
and a giant slide; a man selling

ice cream—at which point I stopped,
realizing I pretty much was rewriting

the lyrics of Chicago's 1972 hit single
"Saturday in the Park," and I probably

wouldn't be able to get the song
out of my head the rest of the day

(I was right—it wouldn't go away).

———————————————

Tonight I made it to the second round
of a spelling bee at a Nob Hill bar,

Café Royale, thwarted by *pompadour*
("We were just listening to the Everly

Brothers, & they have ridiculous pomp-
adours," my bandmates Brian and Allison

texted in solidarity after my whiny message
about losing the bee to competitors who got

easier words like *hierarchy* and *adjunct*
in the same round); at the corner of

Leavenworth and Pine, on the way
to Café Royale, hours before Millicent

Collins's morose episode introduction
("And this night, a night which began

with bright moonlight, has turned dark,
and a woman has thrown herself from

a cliff, the victim of a witch's curse"),
Liz and I ran into my favorite Bay Area

protestor, Frank Chu—my cousin Michael
and I interviewed him for our website in 2000

—standing next to a *San Francisco Chronicle*
newspaper box; Frank leaned over to me

like he was sharing a secret and said,
"I told Charles Osgood they promised

my family they'd be movie stars, and he said
they're guiltied across thousands of galaxies"

(his picket sign, as always, plastered with
urgent, all-cap, non-sequitur exhortations:

BROWNWORTH   KATROKILIANS OF
POPULATIONS   ABC: PETROJRENIKUL

INTERGALACTIC THEORETICS   FITROGRENICAL).

———————————

The trial of Victoria Winters begins,
and already it feels like a cross between

Kafka and a secret American military
tribunal in Guantanamo: Rev. Trask

accuses Victoria's lawyer of witchcraft
because the man is defending Victoria

against the charge of witchcraft.

———————————

Joshua's son is a vampire and his sister
a dimwitted fundamentalist scold;

his wife drinks way too much sherry
and he steadfastly refuses to allow her

to testify at the trial of an accused witch;
his niece just tried to stab her ex-lover

who had proposed to her while married
to someone else—if not for the gaudy

sets and elegant period costumes,
I'd swear the Collins family was

nothing but *True Blood* trailer trash.

———————————

No one pays attention to a servant
who talks in a grubby, alehouse slur,

but Ben Stokes is right: you don't belong
in a graveyard this time of night if you

hear voices. "Perhaps you will allow me
to return to my grave for the rest of eternity,"

Josette says to Barnabas—she's honed
a wicked sense of irony since jumping

from Widows' Hill—chastising the vampire
for raising her from the dead, her face rotting

but no dirt or slime on her white burial gown
(add corpse putrefaction to the list of horrors

I learned as a child from *Dark Shadows*).

_____

Barnabas stirs in his casket in the Old
House basement (close-up of Abigail

Collins watching the coffin lid lifted
from the inside by her undead nephew)

one day after bringing Josette back
from the dead—Kathryn Leigh Scott,

as Josette, walking from her character's
grave in a doped-up Thorazine shuffle,

the same listless gait I remember from
Maggie Evans, whom Scott plays in 1967,

when Barnabas tries (and fails)
to make a vampire-bride of Maggie;

inspired by the restless dead of Collinsport,
I returned this weekend to Camp Chesterfield,

the American Spiritualist community
founded in 1886, with Liz, David Trinidad,

and Jeffery Conway, and on July 20,
the day my mother would've turned 87,

she appeared to Rev. Cindy Spencer
during a public message service

in the Chesterfield chapel (we sat with
numerologist Patricia Kennedy, who cares

for the four of us like a psychic grandma),
identifying herself to Rev. Spencer

as "Margie," the nickname everyone
used when she was alive instead of

calling her "Margaret" or, yes, "Maggie";
it's time to open all the graves—Barnabas,

Josette, and now Margie Trigilio: possessed
in shamanic thrall by my mother, Rev. Spencer

began to mimic my drumming, her arms
and wrists snapping as if she sat behind

a clairvoyant drum kit, and told me
to change the time signature by which

I live (no such thing as coincidence,
I'd been playing one of my band's newest

songs in my head before the service,
breaking down the musical notation

to figure out if the song should be in 5/4
time instead of 4/4)—"you change the beat,"

she said, "you change your whole life";
later, eating cream of tomato soup

at a Panera in Chesterfield, David said
he cried when my mother reminded me,

through Rev. Spencer, I used to hold on
tightly to her pointer finger as a toddler

anytime we left the house (immediate flash
of memory, walking with her to the car,

age two, late-August sun's prickly reflection
off the rusted chrome door handle of our

Dodge Dart as I gripped her finger in my
tiny left hand, always excited to leave

the house with my parents and be driven);
"I wanted to cry, too," I said to David—

it's been a decade since I felt her
spectral presence this strongly,

except in dreams—"but I knew if I did,
I'd forget everything my mother was saying."

I'm not as brainy-tough as I thought,
if a stranger in a Spiritualist chapel

in the plains of rural Indiana
can bring my dead mother back,

talking more lucidly than she did after
her stroke—I haven't been able to speak

Italian since she died—with everyone frozen
around me like the wooden owls my

brother-in-law whittled at his garage work-
bench in the 1970s; fitting that the eccentric

5/4 opening bass line of Jethro Tull's
"Living in the Past" comes to mind

(definitely not hip to make allusions
to prog rock in a goth poem, but I can't

help myself—once, in a graduate school
workshop, I brought a poem to class

that unironically, I confess, appropriated
lines from *Thick as a Brick*), but this only

confuses me more, since I'm actually trying
to live in the present moment of the past,

even though I've been mired in the past,
in 1795, for 67 episodes, and tonight

Little David, the psychic child, returns
as sensitive Daniel Collins, Millicent's little

brother, and immediately is preyed upon
by Rev. Trask, as he is by Barnabas

in the twentieth century (all children are
unsafe in Collinsport, no matter what

millennium they live in): "You have been
touched by the Devil," the witchfinder tells

frightened Little Daniel, "a devil was with
you daily, teaching you, playing with you—

your only hope is to talk with me."

———————————

Fifteenth anniversary of my move from
Boston to Chicago, and Victoria Winters's

lawyer, Peter Bradford, flubs his lines
eight times in one episode, an average

of one mistake every 2½ minutes.
"I'm afraid that physical love is beyond

my comprehension," Rev. Trask says,
which helps explain the erotic zeal

he's brought to Victoria's tribunal.

———————————

The courtroom chandelier casts a spiked
shadow—a Statue of Liberty tiara—

behind Victoria's head, and Episode 435
reveals two witnesses who can save her:

a neurotic ex-convict and a dead man who
sleeps by day in a coffin in his basement.

Only 998 more episodes to go in this poem;
now that I've dipped below 1,000, it feels

less like an impossible object, though
the end of the poem is still unimaginable

as my own death (I'm a future dead
person, but I want to finish the poem

before I'm tucked into my coffin):
I'm a long way from being done

with Ben Stokes's mangy flop of hair,
Peter Bradford in a tailored peacoat

and oversize green seafaring sweater,
more talk of ghosts, the crack of soundstage

foliage, stock nightingale trills piped
into a clearing near Eagle Hill Cemetery,

the witch Angelique vanishing from
her grave (like nearly everyone else

who died in Collinwood in late 1795,
except Sarah, who will wait 172 years

before rising again, as Ghost Girl, in 1967).

———————————

"When I was a child, I used to have
nightmares all the time"—me, too,

Victoria, no matter how diligently
I hunched my shoulders before

going to sleep—"in fact, I got so used to
the nightmares I became curious about them"

—maybe you'll write a poem about your
curiosity, Victoria, but I'm warning you

right now it'll take 1,225 episodes to finish—
"I'd be dreaming something awful and then

suddenly I'd realize it was only a dream"
—no such mercy for me, Victoria,

as Barnabas crawled down the shingles
of my house, wolf's-head cane in hand—

"instead of waking myself up, I'd keep on
dreaming, right until that final second just

before the car crashed or the monster
caught me"—his cane smashing my

bedroom window, loud enough to wake
my parents, who rushed into my room

but couldn't help because this was a vampire,
not some ordinary mortal—"and then,

and only then, I'd wake myself up."

_____

After another trip to the sherry decanter
Naomi stutters through her soliloquy,

Rears back and slaps Rev. Trask—
"Don't you ever talk to me

Away that way that way again,"
She says (later, another nightmare-

Inducing Barnabas close-up at the window,
Creepy slant-rhyme grin and menacing stare).

Leap Day, 1968: MLK's, RFK's killings
Around the corner, the Tet Offensive

A month old, Ben Stokes swilling
Rum at The Eagle—an unimpressive

18th-century Blue Whale knockoff—
Drinking to forget Barnabas's "Cask

Of Amontillado" torture (walled-off
Victim encased in brick) of Rev. Trask.

The vampire orders Ben not to panic.

_____

My god, it's still 1795, the year Coleridge
meets Wordsworth; Blake publishes

The Book of Los; Haydn's "Drumroll"
symphony premieres; the first

recorded meteorite in modern history
falls in Yorkshire, England; the pencil

lead is patented (in France, by Nicolas-
Jacques Conté); de Sade's *Philosophy*

in the Bedroom is published; Keats is born;
and the streetwalker Maude Browning

("Maudie"), strangled by Barnabas, is found
dead on Rev. Trask's spartan bed, the day

after she desperately pounded on a door
near the waterfront (Barnabas on her heels),

screaming, "Help, someone help me,
someone"—my very words the night

I woke in a pitch-black room, sleepwalking
after another *Dark Shadows* nightmare,

too disoriented to realize it was the bedroom
I shared with my brother, feeling for

the light switch on the wall, eventually
so confused by the total darkness

I yelled Maudie's exact words so my parents
could rescue me before the vampire

walked out of the wall to bite my neck.

———————————

Barnabas entombs Rev. Trask brick
by brick in the Old House basement:

let me guess, did Lela Swift, queen
of the premature burial trope, convince

director John Sedwick we needed
a final shot from Trask's POV

as the vampire laid the final brick?
"Why," Millicent asks, "do people

insist on telling me that Barnabas is
dead?" What do you think, Naomi,

is it even worth asking Millicent why
she snuck out after dark, hugging

a large pistol case? Did Navy Lt.
Nathan Forbes really just brandish

Barnabas's wolf's-head cane from
his pelvis and swing it in Joshua's face

like a walloping wolf's-head erection?

———————————

Does it still count as "Oedipal" if
the son is already dead and climbs

out of a coffin to kill his father?

———————————

Naomi enters stage left and promptly
bumps Daniel Collins—too much

sherry, or did Little Daniel's child-
sized, psychedelic, Pre-Raphaelite

smoking jacket just blow her mind?
Is the shadow on the wall of Millicent's

bedroom an enormous grasshopper
or a hunched stagehand wearing

bulky headphones—and should I
worry that Little Daniel is now

sauntering around the Great House
wrapped in a facsimile of Barnabas's

Inverness cape? Do I quote what
Navy Lt. Nathan Forbes just asked

Millicent ("Now, who do you think
lives up there, an imprisoned poet

languishing with love?") or should
I give up trying to extract a usable

question from Episode 449?

_____

Countess du Prés summons an ancient
psychic in black mourning dress and

gloomy head scarf who looks exactly like
a neighbor of mine from 21 years ago,

when I lived in Boston's North End;
disturbed by her black hood scarf,

jaundiced skin, omniscient smirk,
I nicknamed her the Angel of Death,

convinced she was staring straight into
my astral body when we'd see each other

at the Hanover Street 7-11; be careful,
Joshua, if you hold eye contact too long,

she'll ask you to translate her lottery tickets
into Italian (painful watching her mouth sag

when I explained she wasn't holding
a winner); leaning against Barnabas's

coffin, a burning candle on the lid,
lightning flash against the stained glass

window behind her, the Angel of Death—
"Bathia Mapes," she's apparently called

(please, someone, put together a death
metal band and name it "Bathia Mapes")—

forgets her line: six seconds of dead air,
then a stagehand shouts it off camera:

Then go to the house of the curse.
"Barnabas—is alive," Naomi says,

interrupted by a thunderclap, the night
I read at Innisfree Bookstore in Boulder,

just two weeks after eight straight days
of biblical rainfall flooded their city,

and the fourth consecutive episode
featuring constant sound-effect thunder

(with no rain) in haunted Collinsport.

2.

There is no rest for those who live in the Great House at Collinwood, for a new terror has come into their lives. Mysterious and unexplainable things are happening, events which make no sense but must be part of some grand, evil plan.

No ideas but in things—in a low-budget
psychotronic pinwheel filmed with

a Vaseline-smeared lens; in a 28-second
dream of a mystery man (shot from

the neck down) in black satin priest
robes pulling on a pair of white gloves

leaning over an unvarnished coffin;
in a backwards tracking shot that reveals

the dream-villain is Navy Lt. Nathan
Forbes wrapping gloved hands around

Little Daniel's neck (poor David Henesy,
trying to act startled and petrified as his

character is choked—his lips betray
him, curl into a nervous smile); no ideas

but in things like the Fiestaware bowl
(color: Flamingo) of pad siew that Liz

and I shared tonight in our apartment
with my ex-wife, Shelly, and her boyfriend,

Nick—first time I've seen Shelly since
2008, three years before I began this poem—

and while gripping a noodle with
my chopsticks, rolling up particulars

to make them general, eating takeout
from the same Thai restaurant, Nori,

that Shelly and I used to order from
(called Blue Elephant back then),

I suddenly couldn't find a boundary
where my body ended and the other

bodies in the room began—the invisible
veil that separates me from everyone else,

the illusion I'm "me" and they're "others,"
was gone: I shared a home with Shelly

for 15 years, but now she was a visitor
in my home, just a half mile south of where

we lived in 2008, when, in tears, we packed
her car and she drove away from Chicago

for good; she's lived in Tucson with Nick
since 2012: he passed tofu-and-cabbage

spring rolls across my dining room
table to the person, me, who moved

to Chicago with his girlfriend, my wife
at the time, in 1998 (where our marriage

collapsed—we made a lot of trouble for
each other); I met Liz in 2009 and we

married in 2011, when I was barely three
pages into this poem: she passed a bowl

of steaming edamame to Shelly and we all
made plans for a winter 2014 Arizona trip,

the four of us gathered around like family.

———————————————

An episode so dull and plodding
I distracted myself inventing new

time-travel paradoxes for Victoria
Winters's journey from 1967 to 1795:

if she doesn't save Little Daniel from
homicidal Navy Lt. Nathan Forbes,

she'll be unemployed when (if?) she
returns to the twentieth century—

the boy won't grow up to sire multiple
generations of the Collins family,

which means no descendants in 1966
to bring her to Collinwood as governess

for Little David, the psychic child.

———————————

In downtown Iowa City, back in my room,
the Hotel Vetro, after a Halloween reading

with David Trinidad—the Strange Cage
reading series, curated by indefatigable

former student Russell Jaffe, in costume
tonight as a judo master, a wrestling

helmet protecting his head and ears
(most of the audience dressed as witches

and ghouls, like we were on the set
of *Dark Shadows*, as I read from Book 1,

the 1967 plotline); David and I chose not to
watch Anne Rice—*Interview with the Vampire*—

interviewed on Craig Ferguson's late-night
talk show, and cued up Episode 455 instead:

Little Daniel is chased into Eagle Hill
Cemetery by a Danny Bonaduce look-alike

(The Partridge Family's pudgy, pubescent
bassist who played his instrument like a bored

bookstore clerk)—"He's after me,"
Little Daniel says to Victoria, who's

hiding in the secret room of the Collins
tomb from a mob that wants to hang her

for witchcraft, "and he's in the graveyard
now." Maybe Victoria is just delirious

from the gunshot wound she suffered during
her prison break, but this is the second

consecutive episode she slipped and called
Little Daniel "David"; her mistake, it seems,

is contagious: Naomi refers to him as
"David" in the same conversation,

and again later, a third time, talking
at the foot of the Great House

staircase to Daniel/David's nemesis,
Navy Lt. Nathan Forbes, who strangled

the future psychic child in the dream
sequence that begins this section

of the poem; "You should start calling him
Daniel-David," said David T. on the phone

a few days later (it's possible he said this
just to get mentioned in the poem again;

he knows I'll write about anyone who
gives me vampiric gifts—*Dark Shadows*

trading cards from former thesis student
Jacob Victorine, classic 1970s Gold Key

Dark Shadows comics from bandmate
Brian Cremins—or anyone who, like

Mary Cross and Lisa Janssen, tells me
stories of watching *Dark Shadows* every

day as children with *their* mothers, too).

———————————

"Mistah Barnabas is under some kind
of terrible curse," Ben Stokes says

to Naomi (me, too, rotting away for
92 consecutive episodes in 1795).

Goth rock alert—I'd give anything to hear
Blixa Bargeld sing Naomi Collins's line

accompanied by variable-speed power
drills and metal rods playing the ribs

of a shopping cart like strings on a harp:
"There was so very little meaning

to our lives before tonight," she says,
"and now there is none—we exist,

that's all." No longer any need for a doctor,
Barnabas; your mother (which is Naomi)

is dead—she left a quill-penned suicide note
for Joshua and struck 1920s poses at the moon

while draining a goblet of poisoned
sherry. I should be proud of myself

for slipping two of my favorite
passages from Ginsberg's "Kaddish"

into the previous sentence (to mark
the 250th episode I've watched for

this poem), but now, on the verge
of Thanksgiving 2013, I'm thinking

morosely of the holiday—"Kaddish"
recalling, as it often does, my mother's

breakdowns and whiplash bipolar swings;
her pained head: the Wednesday before

Thanksgiving, odor of pumpkin and clover
everywhere in our tiny home, pretty

much the only day of the year she could
speak without running out of breath—

no tightness in her chest, no unnamable
terrors and high blood pressure choking

her words; my mother who once confessed
to me that she recalled nothing from her life

before age 15—my mother with no childhood
memories whom I elegize in this gigantic

poem that wouldn't exist without
my uncannily precise, pre-linguistic

recollections of watching a television
soap with her every day in our living

room; my mother (which is Margaret),
who sat with me in front of our TV

on 3/29/68 as Barnabas Collins's father
chained him inside a coffin and the good

townsfolk of Collinsport hanged Victoria
Winters for acts of witchcraft actually

committed by Barnabas's wife, Angelique
(we watched the rope swing, heard it

creak under the weight of Victoria's
body choking to death on the soundstage

gallows, black hood covering her head);
Mothers of America, let your kids go

to the movies—get them out of the house
so they don't have to see a TV show

that routinely buries its characters
alive and now just executed an innocent

woman in slow, excruciating detail.

———————————————

After 95 episodes in 1795, the show
stumbles back into the 20th century:

"During one tick of a clock in 1968,
months have passed in 1795," Carolyn

says in Episode 461's introduction—
but the last time the antique grandfather

clock in the Great House parlor actually
ticked was in 1967, during the séance

that transported Victoria into 1795
(clearly, the show's writers assume

viewers on April 1, 1968, have forgotten
that 1967 was literally a second ago—

or is the passage of time in Collinsport
just an April Fool's joke?); don't worry,

Victoria Winters isn't dead: at the last
moment she switched places with

Phyllis Wick, an 18th-century woman
who, later, is taken dead from the gallows

but mistakenly blinks when the executioner
removes her hood. Look, I'm not asking for

tea and scones, but I did expect a quieter
transition back into the 20th century:

the ghost of Jeremiah Collins, killed
in a duel with Barnabas in 1795, claws

himself from the grave 173 years later
(decomposed left eyeball hanging from

its socket, blood-stained bandages wrapped
around his head like a moldering turban)

and warns Victoria that Barnabas
plans to kill her; suddenly Dr. Hoffman

reappears in Collinwood sporting a shorn,
androgynous hairdo (tough to figure out

whether she's flirting with Barnabas or just
hamming up her reaction shots again)—

but I can't concentrate on what the two
are saying (I think he's blackmailing her)

because the Old House fountain's
incessant background tinkling

sounds like someone peeing in a urinal.

_____

"I advise you to try charming the vice
president of the Collinsport Savings Bank

and leave me alone—I am, from your
point of view, disgustingly normal,"

Lawyer Peterson says to Carolyn,
after she turns down his offer

to go to a ball game in Bangor.

_____

Watching the 4/4/68 episode with Liz
in Madison, Wisconsin, I wrote down

every object we saw in the final scene—
Barnabas's eighteenth-century portrait,

a mantelpiece clock below the painting
(7:20 p.m. in Collinwood), 17 candles,

two faded pink pillars, a pair of gloomy
emerald curtains, four candelabra,

a sconce mirror reflecting one of the candles,
the vampire's Inverness cape hanging

from a coatrack, Dr. Hoffman's drag wig
and false lashes so big they cover each

eye like an awning—as if hoarding these
objects in my notebook (pausing the DVD

to count every candle) could make me forget
that three hours after the credits roll, 6:01 p.m.

central time, Martin Luther King is shot
to death by James Earl Ray on a balcony

outside his room at the Lorraine Motel
in Memphis as he prepares to go to dinner.

The next day, James Earl Ray abandons
his Mustang nine blocks from King's

church in Atlanta, then takes a bus
to Cincinnati, transferring from there

to Detroit—but it's business as usual
at ABC: *Dark Shadows* not preempted

for coverage of King's assassination,
and Vicki, driving to the Collins family

tomb with Barnabas, swerves to avoid
her 18th-century lover, Peter Bradford,

who inexplicably stepped from dark
woods into the road and waved at her,

causing the car to crash into a tree.
"I have a certain interest in bizarre

medicine—it's a hobby of mine, actually,"
says Dr. Lang, played by Addison Powell,

the voice of Jeremiah Collins's ghost,
two days after James Earl Ray takes

a cab across the border to Canada,
eventually making it to Europe,

where Scotland Yard will capture
him (on 6/8/68) at Heathrow Airport,

false passport in his hand and loaded
pistol in his pocket, trying to board

a European Airways flight to Brussels.

———————————

A 20-year veteran of *All My Children,*
Liz explains why we've spent so much

time the past two episodes at Barnabas's
bedside with Dr. Lang: "All soap operas

use hospitals for major plot twists:
I can picture the writers sitting around

saying, 'How are we going to expose
Barnabas as a vampire—wait, I know,

let's make him get in a car accident
and the doctors figure out everything

when they can't find his pulse.'"

———————————

"Try to be sensible," Dr. Hoffman
Counsels Vicki, which is probably

The worst remark a shrink could make
To a desperate person trying to erase

Posttraumatic time-travel recollections
Of her own witchcraft trial and execution.

Dr. Lang, this is no way to speak to your
Personal assistant (Jeff Clark, alias Peter

Bradford, who sounds like he's gargling
Every time he speaks, and who's starting

To believe he and Vicki really were doomed
Lovers on the gallows, hands tied, black hoods

Over their heads, back in 1795): "Why do
You use the word *sanitarium*—can't you

Say the words *institution for the criminally
Insane*?" Watching Episode 470 with Liz

And Kevin Cassell, who's visiting us this week
From Michigan ("I bought potato chips to eat

During *Dark Shadows,* is this OK?" he asked):
Vicki's lemon nightgown with elaborate

Flared sleeves billows like a citrus parachute
When she walks down the Great House stairs,

An infantile ribbon (same color) in her hair;
I asked Liz if she was offended that I dared

Rhyme her name and the word "criminally"
Five couplets ago—it's the kind of thinly

Veiled slant rhyme that suits songwriting
More than poetry, like the off rhyme

A few stanzas earlier: "parachute" and "stairs"
(Liz from the other room: "Why should I care—

You're not actually calling me a criminal.")

———————————————

Pouty faced in a two-tones-of-green
Updike turtleneck-blazer combo

and blowing cigarette smoke out
the window (a stagehand coughs

off camera), the Danny Bonaduce
look-alike Victoria Winters shot

to death in 1795 arrives in 20th-century
Collinwood as Harry, mysterious

ne'er-do-well son of Collins family
maid Mrs. Johnson, who makes

her first appearance in 112 episodes.
As Roger inspects Dr. Lang's harpoon

collection, another stagehand goes into
a coughing fit—no one smoking this time;

later, Dr. Lang complains to Barnabas,
the vampire he's treating with occult

injections, that he's tired of all this talk
about witches, curses, and spirits:

"I am a man of *science*," he says, cueing
three more phlegmy off-camera hacks

(even with all the money ABC saved on
clothing—the show's wardrobes provided

by mid-level department store chain
Ohrbach's, who also supplied fashions for

All My Children and *Mister Ed*, the bizarre
talking-horse sitcom—the network refused

to splurge on cough drops for the crew).

————————————

Tonight I marked the one-year anniversary
(4/17/68) of Barnabas's first appearance

brooding over the DVD extras: asked
about fan obsessions, Kathryn Leigh

Scott, who plays Maggie and Josette,
tells the story of a female fan who paid her

dentist to bond fangs to her teeth
("They'll be there *forever*," Scott says,

"but she's a housewife—with two
children") and offhandedly reveals

that some *Dark Shadows* devotees legally
changed their last names to "Collins"—

961 episodes to go, and I'm still worrying
that my multivolume impossible object

is nothing more than a pair of fake
fangs permanently attached to my teeth

("They'll be there *forever*," Scott says,
"but he's a professor—with two cats").

More anxiety today, self-loathing doubt
that composing a poem in 1,225 sentences

over an indefinite number of years—
"writing as an act of radical endurance,"

as I described my project in a recent
interview—is the equivalent of starfuck

body modification; I coped by cheating
the poem's procedural constraint, wrote

this extra sentence about yesterday's
episode: the witch Angelique returns

as Cassandra—green, Manson-girl eyes
matching her dress—blushing bride

of Roger Collins, who eloped with her
(struck by one of Angelique's spells)

after a one-day courtship and now
feels he must defend the whirlwind

romance to his sister, Mrs. Stoddard:
"As far as you're concerned," he says,

an indignant flourish, as always, rising
in his throat, "I should've met an already-

approved widow, one with whom I would've
spent months sipping tea and having dinner

until finally we got to know each other
so well that we got *bored to death* with

each other—and then we would marry."

After 95 episodes in 1795 playing
Ben Stokes, earnest and illiterate

18th-century Collins family servant,
Thayer David swaggers around

Collinsport in 1968 as an art history
professor who wears a monocle

(I couldn't make this up if I tried);
his advanced graduate degrees can't

prevent him from flubbing his lines
—did he really just call his own book

an essay?—and, yes, of course, you
may see the talisman, Barnabas,

once Professor Stokes sees the witch.

————————————

Checking my email before bed (after
a night of multiple rewinds to confirm

I actually saw a stagehand tap a yellow
wrench against a machine buzzing

in Dr. Lang's Frankenstein laboratory),
I found a message from an old friend,

Dave Polster, who used to sit with me
under the giant oaks on the Kent State

campus—one of which shielded Alan
Canfora on 5/4/70, when the National Guard

opened fire on unarmed student protestors
(ducking behind the tree saved his life)—

smoking cigarettes after our American
Transcendentalism class, digging our

bare feet into prickly grass; Dave and I
decided Emerson's maxim, "Each age,

it is found, must write its own books"
was a prophetic call for us to make

zines and comics, which we did, of course,
giving them away at cafés and record stores

(the best we could do to endure the horrifying
Reagan '80s); Dave's email was an exuberant

response to the first volume of this poem,
published last month ("Very haunting,"

he wrote, "your poor hunched shoulders!"),
and if the book receives no other reviews,

at least I'll know my words made a visceral
imprint on someone—though I fear I've

unleashed a vampire on friends and family,
as Willie Loomis did on 4/17/67, when he broke

Barnabas Collins from his grave and exposed
the bare neck and jugular of rural 20th-century

Maine to the hungry 207-year-old vampire:
"After reading your poem last night,"

Dave wrote, "I awoke this morning and found
a fucking bat sleeping on a window blind inside

our living room; I tried to grab it, but the thing
woke up and extended its vampire bat wings

and swooped and swooped and swooped
all over our house, spreading terror to my

family and me—was it Barnabas?"

———————————————

"Staring at the flame somehow makes me
forget about my troubles," says Cassandra,

alias the witch Angelique, to Lawyer
Peterson. Perhaps it also made her miss

her cue to walk down the Great House
staircase in a sleeveless minidress

and launch the scariest plot twist imaginable
for an insomniac toddler who saw himself

as Maggie Evans, the woman stalked
by the same vampire he was convinced

lived inside the walls of his own house
and came out at night to torment him

in his sleep: "Let the dream-curse begin
this night," the witch Cassandra says,

"it will go deep into the sleeping mind
of Maggie Evans and she will be the first

to know the fear that is carried with it."

———————————————

Alexandra Moltke (Victoria Winters)
introduces tonight's episode, her voice

burdened, as usual, by goth-gloom
hyperbole: "The same unblinking moon"—

not a *blinking* moon, flashing on and off,
no satellite strobe light—"that Victoria

Winters saw shining on Collinwood
in her terror-ridden journey into the past

shines this night over the great House by
the Sea, but the moon, and Collinwood itself,

are not the only survivors from the past."
Not to be outdone, Cassandra takes

her own shot at a moony introduction
in the next episode: "A silent moon

shines over the Great House in Collin-
wood, a silent observer to all the terrors,

past and present, that have visited
the Collins family" (160 more episodes

to go until the show's first werewolf).

—————————————————

In 1966, Beach Boy Brian Wilson
arrives late for a showing of John

Frankenheimer's sci-fi thriller, *Seconds*,
at a Los Angeles theater; as he seats

himself, the first words he hears from
the screen are "Hello, Mr. Wilson"

(spoken to Rock Hudson's character, Tony
Wilson), which convinces the notoriously

drugged-out and paranoid Brian that
the film is secretly based on his life—

"Even the beach was in it," he says later,
"a whole thing about the beach, it was

my whole life right there on the screen"
(eventually, he blames Phil Spector

and his "mind gangsters" for the movie)—
leaving him so scared, he won't see

another film until *E.T. the Extra-Terrestrial*:
two years after Wilson's self-absorbed

cinematic trauma, I heard the witch
Cassandra call out psychically across

haunted Collinsport to Lawyer Peterson,
"I need you, Tony—if you're asleep,

wake yourself, hear me and know you
must come"; later, when Peterson tries

to walk away from her, at Collinwood's
tinkling pee-pee fountain, Cassandra

dares Little Tony, the not-so-psychic child,
to sleep soundly without fear of vampires

and witches: "Tony, were you *leaving*"
—I remember those witchy green eyes!—

"oh, you must *never* try to do that again."

———————————————

At a four-day writing conference in Seattle,
drunk on glad-handy-dandy schmoozing,

dizzy from the neediness of 13,000 writers
making ourselves visible all at once—

the four days each year we pretend
we're relevant—I'm watching the episode

that aired on Walpurgisnacht, the annual
Central and Northern European witch-

celebration holiday (April 30, also the date
Bram Stoker's short story "Dracula's Guest"

takes place); even on supernatural holidays,
the sets are cheap—the walls shaking when

Jeff Clark, surrounded by clouds of nocturnal
dry ice, pulls the knob of a door that locked

behind him; and later, after tonight's
episode, I discovered why we haven't

seen the decrepit, cobwebbed interior
of the Old House since Victoria Winters

returned from 1795: in the DVD extras,
director Lela Swift, queen of the premature

burial trope, tells a story about the time
she sent away the Old House set for minor

repairs, only to find out later that
someone from ABC mistakenly

took it to the dump to be burned.

———————————————

The return of Willie Loomis: he's still
petrified, jittery—still Barnabas's bottom

even after a 151-episode break from his
master (the vampire doesn't seem like much

of a sadist, though, when he gets dreamy-
eyed and tongue-tied every other sentence).

Everything juicy enough for my sentence
is hazardous, Willie, to your fragile psyche; still

manipulated by Dr. Lang's Faustian dream,
you can a) work yourself up from the bottom,

like a soap opera Igor, and help Lang mash
together a Frankenstein monster from his

grave-robbed booty, or b) simply refuse his
demand for help and one day find yourself sent

back to the asylum (*Enough! or Too much!*
as Blake might describe such choices)—still,

the nuthouse would spare you the rock-bottom
cheesy fog-machine special effects of the dream-

curse unfolding like a dull serial poem: dreaming
of fake fog swirling around three closed doors (he's

obviously going to open them all), Lang is bottoming
out: he lost the rational cool needed to create sentience

from dead matter, and despite his brilliance, he's still
mired in the dream-curse, which riffs too much

off *Let's Make a Deal* to be scary—not much
suspense, knowing that in each new dream,

the victim will choose to open *all* the doors. Still,
Lang says, he's always found a way to return to his

work after a nightmare (later, I add a sentence
about how quickly Dr. Hoffman got to the bottom

of Lang's dream: she's a shrink, of course, bottom
line; though she can't act, I'm impressed by how much

she sounds like a real therapist—each sentence
of exegesis as elegant as *The Interpretation of Dreams*).

Dr. Lang might be on the verge of creating life, but he
can't come up with a more original name for the still-

inert man than "Adam"? He's trying too hard to instill
operatic tragedy in what's, at bottom, predictable as this

sestina: six end-words every stanza like a recurring dream.

Celebrating Michael Trigilio and Trish
Stone's wedding at Pittsburgh's Mattress

Factory museum, where the transcendent
extravaganza of red dots in Yayoi Kusama's

Repetitive Vision made me light-headed:
Professor Stokes, monocled art historian

and student of the occult, keeps a safe
distance from Sam Evans's maudlin

paintings, walks past Sam's canvases
like they were clutter in a hoarder's nest—

can we finally stop pretending Sam
is the show's tortured artist-in-residence?

"I have too much work to do to be bothered
with dreams," says Collins family maid

Mrs. Johnson (pretty much what Ted Kooser
tells me every time I slog through his flat,

utilitarian little poems); poor Little David
returns from a 32-episode absence—sporting

a green Nehru jacket too groovy for dark
and tragic Collinwood—only to find Lawyer

Peterson and the witch Cassandra, the psychic
child's new stepmother, crawling over each other

at the gazebo in yet another awkwardly
feral *Dark Shadows* make-out session.

After a reading in Fort Wayne organized
by George Kalamaras—still tasting

the deliciously sour jolt of the kimchi
pie we shared at lunch—I wish tonight's

episode introduction could actually
describe the opening scene of a lost

Guy Maddin film: "On this night,
a woman has sought refuge in the house

of a dead doctor." In late Dr. Lang's
Frankenstein laboratory, his creature

on the verge of life (corpse-stitched
body strapped to the operating table,

surrounded by portentous beakers and
glass tubes gurgling like water bongs),

Dr. Hoffman flails at the laboratory
control panel knobs and levers as if

she's piloting a doomed submarine.

———————————————

If only my childhood *Dark Shadows*
nightmares could have been so obviously

staged as the terrors of Cassandra's
dream-curse: two episodes ago,

Dr. Hoffman's screeching, self-conscious
overacting (every scrape is a hemorrhage

for actress Grayson Hall) actually
made it easier to spot the stagehand

poised in the blacked-out backdrop
next to the dream-guillotine and the silver

outline of a bucket on the other side
of the dream-door spewing dry ice

all over the soundstage; then tonight,
Mrs. Johnson's turn, opening the next

dream-door, revealing cheap stock footage
(like something out of Mutual of Omaha's

Wild Kingdom) shot in a cave: hanging bats
superimposed on the open threshold

of the door—the bats look startled,
as if Mrs. Johnson just caught them

masturbating, which makes their twitching
fox faces and tiny, earnest eyes adorable

rather than terrifying; later tonight,
my second *Dark Shadows* dream since

I began this project nearly three years ago:
in the dream, Liz says, "Don't leave Barnabas

home alone with our roommates"—
for some reason, we share our home

with others in this dream—"he'll suck
their blood, kill them all, and when you

get home, he'll give you that innocent
wide-eyed look that says, 'I can't help

biting people's necks—it's my nature.'"

———————————

Barnabas keeps so many secrets
from the citizens of Collinsport

(he's a vampire cursed by the witch
Cassandra, who went by the name

Angelique when she and Barnabas lived
in the 18th century; he killed Dr. Woodard,

with Dr. Hoffman's help; he imprisoned
Maggie Evans in a basement dungeon

because she refused to become his vampire-
wife; and he helped create a Frankenstein

monster named Adam in a harebrained
scheme to transfer Angelique's curse)

it's no wonder the vampire can't
deliver his lines without stumbling:

"Your only safety is to talk to Adam,"
he says to Willie Loomis, "keep an eye

on him—talk to him and be friendly
and nothing will have given you

any fear either from him or from me."
Dr. Hoffman narrates tonight's episode

introduction, remarking that "another day
comes to a quiet close at Collinwood"

—an accurate enough preview, if I
ignore gigantic Adam, collaged from

dead body parts, who tromps around
Collinwood with no impulse control,

quick-tempered and babbling like
an agitated infant. Watching Adam

learn language through painstaking
imitations of Barnabas's lurching

soliloquies, I've lost track of how far
the plot has strayed from its source,

Mary Shelley's *Frankenstein,* whose
lonely monster picked up language

from, among other books, a discarded
copy of *Paradise Lost* (better to reign

in hell than botch your lines in heaven);
I learned to read the same year, age two,

that Adam came to life on Dr. Lang's
operating table, a condition called hyperlexia

in which children somehow learn
to decode words on their own, without

any formal instruction on how to read;
my parents propped me on the kitchen

counter at family gatherings and gave me
copies of *Time* and *Newsweek* to read aloud

to everyone like a circus monkey riding
a bicycle: I don't remember the articles—

it was 1968, and I'm sure many of them
were about Vietnam, where my brother

Frank was assigned to a combat platoon—
but I do recall, age four, a year before *Dark*

Shadows was canceled, the first newspaper
story that ever made me angry: a report

on the Kent State murders in the *Erie Daily*
Times, my father preemptively telling me

the protesting students were to blame
for being shot in the head, lungs, chest,

neck, back, wrist, and stomach (four
dead and nine wounded, one paralyzed)

even though they were unarmed.

———————————————

The camera lingers on the sculpture
in the Great House foyer longer

than I've ever seen before, and finally
I can make out some of the details—

not sure, but I think it's a shirtless
worker shoveling peat in a bog;

later, Adam brushes past a clump
of thick bushes on the grounds

of the Collinwood estate and a top-
heavy foliage prop falls like a potted

plant, revealing its square, wooden base
(Robert Duncan and his partner, Jess,

were devoted fans of *Dark Shadows*
and watched the show every afternoon,

but no matter how often they permitted
themselves to return to the overgrown

forest surrounding Collinwood, it was
always a scene made up by the mind,

a made place ready to topple).

———————————————

Joe, please work harder to convince
Maggie to remove her earrings—

each time the camera zooms in,
we're forced to endure the cloying

ice-cream-truck melody of Josette's
eighteenth-century music box (bonus:

left earring falls out in mid-argument,
Maggie tries to cover it with her hand).

Maggie's father, Sam Evans, returns
after a 103-episode absence, 10 pounds

heavier and sporting a handlebar
mustache, painting a rickety fishing

boat with a bizarre banana-yellow
prow: despite the swooping Dalí

'stache, he's still a lousy artist.

———————————————

"A month ago, I might've been worth
falling in love with," Lawyer Peterson

says to the back of Carolyn's neck—
the classic soap opera shot Liz noticed

in Episode 288—"now I'm not so sure."

———————————————

Today, May 4, 2014, the 44th anniversary
of the Kent State murders, I'm watching

Episode 500 and still wondering why
Sam Evans wasn't suspicious yesterday

when the woman rapping at his door
after midnight (in a thunderstorm)

concealed her face beneath a druid's hood;
earlier this morning, at breakfast, scrolling

through a Flickr page of images from
Kent State's 1987 Remembrance Day

ceremony, I found a photograph of myself
among the crowd of spectators sitting

on the Commons, the grassy campus
quad, my denim backpack next to me

—I didn't know the photo existed,
and I'd forgotten the old black-and-red

flannel I'm wearing in the picture—
steps from the campus Victory Bell,

originally rung after football wins but used
in the '60s to summon the dorms for antiwar

rallies, where students buried a copy
of the U.S. Constitution on May 4, 1970

(they were fired upon a half hour later),
protesting Nixon's invasion of Cambodia;

I'm alone in the photo, saving a spot
for Dave Polster (who, earlier this year,

chased a bat from his home after
falling asleep reading Book I

of this poem), listening to civil rights
icon Julian Bond speak from the stage

erected next to the Bell for the ceremony:
I can tell from my constipated squint

and pursed lips in the picture that I'm
holding back tears, though I remember

letting it rip, wide-open sobbing,
when Sarah and Martin Scheuer

took the podium and spoke about
their daughter, Sandra, who was shot

in the neck May 4, 1970, by a National
Guard soldier as she walked through

the Prentice Hall parking lot to her
Speech class and, after a series of

convulsions, died from loss of blood.

———————————

Adam, hiding behind soundstage foliage
shivering and drenched, fleeing the Old

House after trying to strangle Barnabas:
perhaps the first time I've seen anyone wet

during a *Dark Shadows* thunderstorm.

———————————

Late afternoon in May, Chicago finally
blooming after its coldest winter in

history—say the phrase "Polar Vortex"
to Chicagoans, watch our bodies clench—

a calm breeze rustles the rubber tree
Liz repotted yesterday, the cats wrestle

in a sunbeam next to the couch, and I
dedicate Carolyn's riddling dream-curse

voice-over to my former thesis student,
Nate Breitling, who died a week ago—

his body found in an alley hours before
we were supposed to meet for coffee,

the cause of death still a mystery:
Nate, whose imagination was wild

and beautifully unhinged like flowering
kudzu, who made the world strange

with poems channeled from someplace
he called "the great gathering in the sky

of tomorrow" ("a no-place," he wrote,
"where Stonehenge is the capital");

I'm struggling to accept we'll never
talk about his work again, no more

conversations that begin with poetry
and somehow drift into tangents about

Henry Kissinger, Watergate, the CIA,
Bobby Fischer's storage facility in Pasadena,

or his post-MFA hike of the Appalachian
Trail with his sister—Nate, you would

throw back your head and laugh if you
could hear Carolyn beckon Willie

into clouds of dream-curse fog (of course,
she's dry, her lime-green sweater puffy

and soft even though Adam carried
her through another *Dark Shadows*

thunderstorm) with faux-incantatory
voice-over so ridiculous even Sam Hall,

husband of Grayson Hall (Dr. Hoffman),
must've laughed at himself when he wrote

the script: "Through sight and sound
and faceless terror, through endless

corridors by trial and error, a head
of blazing light does burn, and one

door leads to the point of return."

Willie's not nervous, Sheriff Patterson—
he's had terrible nightmares ever since

a vampire sprung him from Windcliff
Sanitarium, and he's just curious

how many howling dogs accompanied
you to the Old House this evening.

Adam kidnaps Carolyn, imprisons her
underground in an abandoned root cellar;

a month before my second birthday,
did I really need another buried-

alive plotline to feed my insomnia?

———————————————

On the first Sunday in June, 1968, two
days after today's literal cliffhanger

episode—chased by the police, Adam
jumps off Widows' Hill (I can't help

but wonder if Robert Duncan and Jess
enjoyed the gnostic gloom of the final

scene, Sheriff Patterson and his deputies
walking back one by one from the cliff

in silence, the wind whistling but not
shaking any of the fake foliage, stars

flickering on and off like flashlight bulbs
in the night-sky soundstage backdrop

over Collinwood)—Sirhan Sirhan visits
the Ambassador Hotel in Los Angeles

to hear Robert F. Kennedy give a speech;
later, during his trial, Sirhan described

to defense attorney Grant B. Cooper
how he felt when he saw Bobby standing

on the hotel's outdoor terrace that Sunday
in '68, two days before assassinating him:

"I was really thrilled, sir," he said, adding,
"he looked like a saint to me—I liked him."

Twenty minutes before Valerie Solanas
shoots Andy Warhol (bullet passes

through both lungs, his spleen, stomach,
liver, and esophagus) and six hours

before Sirhan Sirhan watches Bobby
Kennedy give a speech at the El Cortez

Hotel, San Diego (driven to exhaustion
by California's presidential primary

campaign, Kennedy interrupted his
remarks and rushed to a bathroom

to vomit), Mrs. Stoddard introduces
the 6/3/68 episode with her usual grim

statement of the obvious: "It has been
a long, terrifying night at Collinwood."

June 4, 1968: Sirhan Sirhan spends
all day at the San Gabriel Valley

Gun Club, practicing his shooting,
and Professor Stokes, the insufferable

aesthete (still monocled), examines
a porcelain figurine that, at first glance

(my bad eyesight, adjusting to trifocals)
resembles the famous Venus of Willendorf

fertility idol—"How *vulgar* Meissen china
can be," Stokes says, spitting the words

through his gelatinous lips, then urging
Carolyn to fall asleep, surrender to the dream-

curse (she does, and finds her own tombstone
lurking behind one of the foggy dream-doors);

after treating himself to a burger and coffee
at Bob's Big Boy, Sirhan decides to skip

the 8 p.m. meeting of the Ancient Mystical
Order of the Rose Cross (the Rosicrucians)

and returns to the Ambassador Hotel,
home to Bobby Kennedy's California

campaign headquarters, and drinks
at least four Tom Collins cocktails—

he later testified they tasted like lemonade
—and is mesmerized by a teletype machine

tapping out election returns in real time
(Sirhan's adventures in self-hypnosis

included phrases he obsessively copied
over and over in his diary, "RFK must

die" and "pay to the order of"): just past
midnight, June 5, RFK is shot in the hotel's

kitchen pantry, after giving his famous
victory speech—"It's on to Chicago,

and let's win there," he said, saluting
the crowd with a final thumbs-up—

Sirhan emptying all eight bullets in his
pistol, though evidence from the crime

scene suggests that 10 were fired.
I watched the 6/5/68 episode with

my mother as doctors tried to save
Kennedy's life (you're right, Professor

Stokes, the worst part of the dream-
curse is when the victim is "forced

to hear that rather pitiful riddle"):
he died at 1:44 a.m. on 6/6/68,

preempting *Dark Shadows* that day,
succumbing to the fatal head shot

Coroner Thomas Noguchi concluded
came from behind and was so close,

one and a half inches from Kennedy,
it left powder burns on his neck (but

Sirhan shot Bobby from the front,
standing more than three feet away);

35 years later, in 2003, writing a poem
about my failed efforts to use children's

picture books to teach my mother to read
and write again after her stroke, I added

the lesson she learned from both Kennedy
assassinations—"Anthony, all the honest

politicians get shot" (Mrs. Stoddard's
brooding can't hold a candle to my

mother's weary fatalism)—and recalled
her lament every time Ted Kennedy's face

flashed on our television in the late '70s:
"Everybody knows if another Kennedy

runs, Anthony, the Mafia'll get him, too."

———————————

"If you should have a dream which begins
with a knock on the door and a man,

probably Barnabas Collins, gesturing for
you to follow him, please call me at once,"

Professor Stokes advises Sam Evans—
just two weeks shy of my second birthday,

I knew a monocled art historian could
do nothing to protect me from Barnabas,

whose full-time occupation was, simply,
to wait inside the walls of my house

for me to fall asleep, biding his time,
stroking his wolf's-head cane until he

heard the cue to start another round of night
terrors on my dream-curse soundstage;

tonight, a few weeks after my 48th
birthday (thank you, David Trinidad,

for the Barnabas replica onyx ring,
and Brian Cremins and Allison Felus

for *Dark Shadows: Year One,* published by
the same company, Dynamite Entertainment,

that reissued the old 1970s *Vampirella*
comic book series), I'm getting a motion-

sickness headache from the black-and-white
kinescope copy of Episode 509—audio warbling,

video wobbly—the original color tape
missing; I reminded Liz that this episode,

the 300th I've watched for my poem
(I've now spent 100 hours, more than

four complete days of my life, planted
in front of a television or laptop with

Dark Shadows), was recorded June 5, 1968,
the day Bobby Kennedy was shot—

and now she's convinced that someone
from the network pilfered the color

videotape as a gruesome collector's item.

———————————————

"I find cheese always helps me sleep,"
Stokes says to Lawyer Peterson, his voice

raised to the glutted, sybaritic pitch
he also struck at the end of the previous

episode, when he uttered this same
exact phrase—I rewound and played

both for Liz on our second night
in San Francisco, staying in the Mission

District again (when we're not following
the interminable dream-curse plotline,

we're sitting outside Luna Rienne Gallery
in the chilly July sun, watching World Cup

quarterfinal soccer matches with gallery
owners Anthony and Olivia—renting their

upstairs apartment, as we did last year—
and anyone else in the neighborhood

who happens to walk past the television
Anthony mounted above the gallery

doorway that faces 22nd Street)—
but Peterson isn't paying attention,

blathering nonstop about a Coptic
cross as he waits for Stokes to quaff

a glass of sherry he poisoned under
the spell of the witch Cassandra;

Professor Stokes survives, switching
glasses with Lawyer Peterson: "We must

find someone the witch cannot affect,
someone who is already dead," he says

to Dr. Hoffman, as the two summon
the ghost of Rev. Trask, renowned

eighteenth-century witchfinder
Barnabas buried alive inside the wall

of the Old House coffin room in 1796
(later, rattled from raising the dead,

and preoccupied with the drawstring
of his chrome-gray smoking jacket,

Stokes walks onto the set as the credits
roll, then sheepishly backs away from

the camera when he realizes his mistake).

———————————————

The same day Liz observed Dr. Hoffman
can't utter a sentence without stuttering

the first word to make sure you know
her lines carry great dramatic heft—

today Hoffman staggered through
three consecutive sentences this way

("It—it's useless" / "We—we should go" /
"Are—are you ready")—she noticed I walk

with a looser gait in the Bay Area,
a fluid stride, open hips, a jaunty

bounce, pretty much the opposite of what
my methodical, regimented father taught me,

the man whose garage was a temple
devoted to his monkish zeal for division

and classification, where corks and keys
and plastic caps and drills and lids and

Vaseline each had a proper shelf, housed
in bowls he made from the bottoms of two-

liter soda bottles, the contents of each
vessel hand-lettered with Sharpie in block

script on masking tape (a child of the Great
Depression, and a man who served as an MP

in World War II and an auxiliary police officer
when he returned to the States, my father

simply wanted containers for all his things,
which is why the first time I read Foucault's

Discipline and Punish, it felt, forlornly,
like déjà vu), and though my dad taught

the self-control that proved handy later,
when I developed a daily meditation practice—

and useful now, a quarter of the way
through this 1,225-sentence procedural

poem that demands I watch 1,225 episodes
of a daytime soap opera—the price was

my absorption of his mania for order:
I'm embarrassed to admit that last year,

for a multimedia performance my cousin
Michael Trigilio produced, I listed all

the obsessive-compulsive steps required
before I can actually leave the apartment

on any given day, and the total was 39.
After another Saturday at Dolores Park—

eight Hula-Hoopers, a crowd of sunbathers,
a homeless man in an Oakland Raiders

baseball cap asking me if I have weed
(a piece of a cannabis chocolate bar, not

enough to share), and a drum circle of 14
musicians orchestrated by a white couple

in turbans and dashikis who ended
the performance banging a giant gong

—Sam Evans, struck blind by the witch
Cassandra, taps his cane against the floor

of his studio like a distracted woodpecker.

3.

Another day will soon come to an end at Collinwood. And when night comes, a frightening moment from the past will come with it to be relived in all its horror.

Perhaps my childhood nightmares
would've abated if I'd understood

Barnabas actually was dying inside
the walls of the Old House coffin room,

sealed in brick by the ghost of 18th-
century witchfinder Reverend Trask

(I was too afraid of the vampire
to empathize with him—only my

hunched shoulders prevented Barnabas
from stepping out of my bedroom wall

and biting my neck every night);
I plan to call Book 2 of this poem

Inside the Walls of My Own House,
but it's become *The Book of Violence*:

bombs going off at the Boston Marathon
finish line; Barbara Jane Mackle buried

alive; my former boss, Zorba, scalping
his brother's wife; pizza-delivery driver

Brian Wells blown up robbing a bank;
Valerie Solanas shooting Andy Warhol;

Martin Luther King and Bobby Kennedy
assassinated—of course, Book 2's catalog

of brutality isn't complete without
adding one of my earliest memories

of violence, the four students murdered
and nine wounded at Kent State

two years after the *Dark Shadows*
episodes I'm watching now, originally

broadcast in 1968, a year that began with
the utter slaughter of the Tet Offensive

in Vietnam (not that 2014 is much better:
as I write this sentence today, July 31,

a total of 1,254 people have been shot
in Chicago this year, nearly six per day,

so much violence I'm desensitized
to the city's new nickname, "Chiraq").

Brian, Allison, and I play a gig at Sacred
Art Chicago on the 16th anniversary

of my move from Boston, just three
hours after Maggie puts on her enchanted

earrings and hears faint tapping behind
the brick wall of the Old House coffin room

—even though my individual memories
of Boston are clear as ever, their neural

network, my web of New England
recollections, started to atrophy

once I moved to the Midwest; by 1999,
after living a full year in Chicago,

I realized that my once-kinetic mesh
of Boston memories had been absorbed

into a nascent clump of associations
called "Chicago," and the pressure

of living in a strange new city, and
keeping track of this place in memory,

made me almost impossible to live with:
bewildered every day, I walked around

with a constant anger that buzzed
like tinnitus, which, I realize now—

after rereading my journal from a 2009
Boston visit, when I listed all the public

places in the city where my ex-wife
Shelly and I argued (outside the Park

Plaza Hotel, on a cell phone, while she
was visiting family in Ohio; in front of

the Boston Public Library; at the Copley
Square Farmer's Market; over breakfast,

twice, at the Finagle a Bagel on Boylston;
in front of the Arlington Street Unitarian

church; on the Queensberry Street bus
too many times to count; at Truffles candy

shop in the Copley Square mall, where
she once worked, the store now replaced

by a GameStop franchise, though it
survives as a snack cart in the middle

of a high-traffic area near the mall's
information desk; at California Pizza

Kitchen right after the restaurant opened;
in the rain, waiting for the Queensberry bus

to take us to Metropolitan Health Club;
and over lunch at the outdoor café

at Five Hundred Boylston, the same
building that housed fictional law firm

Crane, Poole & Schmidt from the old
television show *Boston Legal*)—is one

more reason for this multivolume
impossible object of a poem: to craft

a new network of neural connections
from memories of every place I've lived,

Chicago/Boston/Kent/Erie/Collinsport.

———————————

Dr. Hoffman stares four seconds
at a sobbing, translucent apparition

before it occurs to her that she's
looking at a ghost. Rev. Trask

sets fire to the witch Cassandra.
She smothers the flames with

her supernatural hands and leaves
the Collins family mausoleum

smoldering on my second birthday.

———————————

"There is one woman who lives
at Collinwood who will not sleep

tonight"—one little insomniac boy,
too, watching that afternoon with

his mother in northwest Pennsylvania—
"Cassandra Collins will lie awake,

thinking about the evil she has set
in motion"—a dream-curse that cursed

my dreams—"thinking about the events
that will soon take place in a hospital

not far away"—Sam Evans will recite
the infantile dream-curse riddle

to Vicki and his daughter, Maggie,
who doesn't believe in witches

though she once was kidnapped
by a vampire and lives in a rural

Maine village where nine people
have experienced the same identical

dream for 42 episodes and counting—
"there, Victoria Winters has answered

the summons of an old and dear friend
who believes he is dying"—cue Collinsport's

blind artist-in-residence Sam Evans finally
croaking (no more banana-prow boat

paintings and sad-clown Norman Mailers!).
Mrs. Stoddard, patron saint of Joy Division:

"We all eventually die, don't we," she says
to Roger, upon learning of Sam's demise:

"I will be next, and I know it'll be soon."

———————————

Is there a *Dark Shadows* spirit guide
looking out for us, manipulating this

mortal world for maximum kitsch, making
sure the first time I watch an episode with

both Liz and David Trinidad (have we
really gone three years and 311 episodes,

104 hours, without sharing one together?)
we're treated to a carnival of blunders:

the camera dips like a canoe during a scene
in the Great House drawing room, Barnabas

forgets his lines ("And for your own
reasons, you remain silent"—clumsy

two-beat pause—"you remain silent
for reasons"), Mrs. Stoddard's raised-

eyebrow inflection looks suspiciously
like a random muscle spasm (too much

sherry?), and Dr. Hoffman speaks every
line with a palsied stutter, trying to talk

to Barnabas while descending the stairs,
which apparently on the set of *Dark*

Shadows is a real challenge, like walking
and chewing bubble gum at the same time

(convinced one of Hoffman's hyperventilated
vowels had lapsed into a Southern accent,

I asked Liz and David to watch a second
time, two weeks later; they heard nothing

unusual, but I still detect an accidental drawl).

———————————

After a reading at Woodland Pattern
Book Center in Milwaukee with

CM Burroughs and Soham Patel,
Dining on chips and salsa, watching

Episode 521 in our hotel room, Liz and I
Fight to stay awake while, inexplicably,

Gangly man-child Adam (Collinwood's
Half-wit Frankenstein monstrosity) launches

Into a nervous recitation of the alphabet:
Jabbing the air with his hands, he goes from

"K" to "M," for some reason skipping the letter
"L," and Prof. Stokes reassures the corpse-stitched

Monster: "I wouldn't be too concerned—'L' is
Not a letter I care very much for": I realize it's

Only 116 episodes since my last abecedarian, but
Professor Stokes's pronouncement, his bizarre

Quarrel with the letter "L" (such a pedant!),
Requires an alphabetical form to rescue today's

Story line from its interminable narrative crawl—
Too soon for another abecedarian, but I trust my

Urge to mimic Adam's parade of phonemes,
Varying them slightly at the start of each line,

While making sure to feature Professor Stokes's
Eccentric vision of a world without the letter "L":

Yes, he's an art historian with a monocle,
Zealously policing the alphabet—how could

I resist the desire to recite my own ABCs.

———————————

I needed a break, after two weeks twisting
Adam's alphabet extravaganza into a strict

poetic form: thank you, Willie Loomis,
for sitting on the floor of the Old House

coffin room and making my sentence
for tonight's episode easy, punning

among the cobwebs with your voice-over—
"This gives me the willies, even *being* here."

Within a day of his arrival in Collinwood,
Nicholas Blair, the witch Angelique's elfin,

androgynous brother, summons the dead
back to life: "You were a blind, overzealous

fanatic," he says to the ghost of Rev. Trask,
"a bigot and a fraud; intolerant, cruel,

and unjust—a man after my own heart"
(I've wished for another thug courtship

since Jason McGuire was killed by Barnabas
248 episodes ago, and Willie, his anxious

pup, was exiled to Windcliff Sanitarium).

———————————

Watching Episode 524 with Joe Harrington
and his partner, MariaAna, during a mid-fall

goth thunderstorm in Lawrence, Kansas:
Jeff Clark dreams it's 1796 and he's Peter

Bradford again (his eighteenth-century
incarnation—Victoria Winters's

Collinsport Gaol guard during her
witchcraft trial), and in the dream

gargly voiced Clark shoots Navy
Lieutenant Nathan Forbes; "You can't

kill me," Forbes says, "I'm already dead,"
the exact words Charles Manson will utter

in court in 1970, which prompts Joe
to observe, "The Tate-LaBianca murders

happen a year after this episode aired—
maybe Manson was watching *Dark Shadows*."

Celebrating World Sake Day (six sugary
shots at Ramen Bowls in Lawrence, my first

sake in 20 years): the camera freezes,
stuck for five seconds in close-up

of Nicholas Blair's hand swirling his
brandy glass—then Roger utters

the word "witch," breaking the spell.
Blair's incantations resurrect his sister,

Angelique/Cassandra, who vanished
seven episodes ago, exorcised from

Collinsport by the ghost of Rev. Trask,
but she doesn't seem very witchy,

returning to this mortal world in a mod,
lime-green evening dress plastered

with gigantic purple butterflies
("Except for the color of her hair,

Cassandra Collins looks exactly like
Angelique," Vicki says later, but I

can't take my eyes off the Peter Max
monstrosity of Cassandra's flare-

sleeved butterfly dress long enough
to pay close attention to her hair).

Best use of the monocle yet: Professor
Stokes clenches it with his right eye,

astonished by Nicholas Blair's
overdramatic entrance in the Great

House drawing room, staring at Blair
as if he were a sprightly little hobbit

just emerged from the bole of a tree.

———————————

The witch Cassandra tricks Vicki into
falling asleep (52 episodes and counting,

ABC simply refuses to let the dream-
curse die), but my mother and I probably

didn't watch today's episode, aired
July 4, 1968—can't imagine my father

postponing our annual holiday cookout
for my mother's soaps—the same day

The Green Berets opened in the U.S.,
starring John Wayne and my cousin,

ex-pro football linebacker Mike Henry,
who made his name in Hollywood

as the 14th actor to play Tarzan;
thinking of Henry's ape-man career

calls to mind the famous pre-production
publicity photo for *Tarzan and the Valley*

of Gold, featuring Henry and Sharon Tate,
originally cast as the movie's female lead—

she lost the part, shortly before shooting
began, to Nancy Kovack, but the Henry/Tate

photo survives, the two of them posing
with a lion, Tate in subdued gray plaid

skirt and black hose (haunting to see
the image and know she would be

slaughtered by the Manson family
four years after the picture taken)

and Henry clad in skimpy loincloth,
Hollywood's only hairy-chested Tarzan;

every time I look at Tate and Henry
(and lion), I remember a photograph

Henry mailed me when I was 10,
a beefcake publicity still of himself

from *Tarzan and the Valley of Gold* (just
a standard Hollywood promo shot,

no way he'd predict that 38 years after
my father asked him for autographed

pictures for my brother and me,
I'd describe this pose as "beefcake"

in a poem about a vampire soap opera),
Henry flexing in loincloth, staring off

camera, a military tank gun barrel
behind him pointed suggestively

upward at a 45-degree angle: *To cousin
Anthony,* he wrote in scratchy cursive

blue ballpoint script, *Love, Mike Henry.*

Joe, it's really not that difficult to understand:
Maggie saw the ghost of a witch whispering

in the ear of sleeping Vicki—who, if she
hadn't been awakened by Maggie's shrieking

(six seconds, four screams, I timed it with
my stopwatch), would've been hypnotized

into sniffing a bottle of enchanted cologne
that would've induced the dream-curse

conjured to kill a vampire 53 episodes ago.
Struggling with my OCD tonight, I lost

track of what Vicki and Barnabas were
saying (his first appearance after an eight-

episode absence), rewinding multiple
times to count the 11 candles in the Old

House parlor—certain it was a bad omen
if all Barnabas's candles added up to a prime

number, like 11, which led me to decide,
spontaneously, that Barnabas's crackling

fireplace was the scene's honorary 12th
candle; eight more candles in the next

parlor scene brought the total to 19,
another prime, and I realized my

brain was stuck in a debilitating loop
(*If I can't make the candles add up to 20,*

I thought—and, no lie, I really believed
this insanity at the time—*then I'm doomed*

to leave the bathroom or kitchen sinks running,
or forget to unplug all the electrical outlets

in the kitchen when I go to bed tonight).
"Willie, we will deal with your mental

aberrations later," Barnabas says, nervously
picking his lips, while in the Great House,

Vicki tries to stay awake all night to avoid
the dream-curse; of course she succumbs,

falls asleep—as I always did—and Barnabas,
cloaked in his Inverness cape, beckons Vicki

amid the swirling dry-ice soundstage fog
of her dream; Vicki screams, "Somebody

help me, somebody, please," nearly my
exact words, as a child, 91 episodes

ago, when I woke, flailing for the light
switch on my pitch-black bedroom wall

after a nightmare caused by Barnabas's
brutal attack on Maude Browning

in 1795 at the Collinsport waterfront.

———————————

Eating glazed donuts and watching *Dark
Shadows* with Michael Trigilio, visiting

this weekend from San Diego, and Liz:
Barnabas slams the door of the Great

House drawing room so hard it jostles
the camera, whose gaze had been frozen—

fixated, really—on the witch Cassandra's
back ("You have to understand, it's live,"

says Dan Curtis, the show's creator,
on the DVD bonus interview I'll watch

the next day, "even though it's shot
on tape, there's no stopping, no turning

back—if somebody dies on the floor,
you have to cut the camera away quickly").

In the first installment of a six-episode stint
as a *Dark Shadows* director, John Weaver jams

three quick-cut, seasick camera angles into
a brief conversation in the Old House parlor

between Barnabas and Dr. Hoffman,
which disorients me so much I can't

count the number of candles in this scene
(more reaction-shot dilemmas for Hoffman,

who, in a wistful, lovelorn moment, gazes at
Barnabas walking up the Great House stairs

and looks instead like she's fighting off nausea).

———————————————

Watching *Dark Shadows* with Liz in Seattle,
a 26th-floor corner room with panoramic

view of storm clouds massing over Elliott Bay
(compliments of the Sheraton: nine months

ago, booked here for the AWP Conference,
I complained about the 45-minute check-in

line and the hotel staff who walked around
offering trays of wine in fluted glasses instead

of staffing the hotel's registration desk—
You were buying our silence with alcohol,

I wrote upon my return to Chicago, another
of my crazed, combative letters to corporations

[my favorite, a five-page, single-spaced
letter to USAir in 1993 about the luggage

they lost when I flew from Boston to Erie
for my 10th high school reunion, demanding

two free tickets to anywhere in the 48 contiguous
states—somehow, omitting Alaska and Hawaii

seemed a reasonable, good-faith negotiating
gesture—which resulted in nothing but a 25%

discount reservation voucher I never used];
the hotel manager replied, "I feel compelled

to invite you back for another experience,
so you can truly enjoy the service Sheraton

and the Sheraton Seattle are known for"):
a drizzly, pink Pacific Northwest sunset

mood-lighting our room, Dr. Hoffman
declares, "Time has been more cruel

to Barnabas than any witch could ever be"
—quite a pulpy gem from writer Gordon

Russell, whom I pictured leaning back
in his desk chair and crossing his arms

after typing this overwrought line,
perversely satisfied that he'd finished

the day's script on a high note (at least
he's about to kill off the dream-curse,

a Rube Goldberg machine of a plotline
triggered when Maggie Evans dreamed

she opened a door onto a skull floating
in dry-ice fog then recounted her dream

to Jeff Clark, who, snoozing in a French
reading chair, saw a guillotine in his dream,

then recounted it to Dr. Lang, who added
a headless man in turtleneck to his dream,

then told it to Dr. Hoffman, who, overacting,
as usual—it's not enough to be dream-cursed,

she has to fall asleep like a drowning woman
gasping for breath—opened a door in her dream

and found a cackling skeleton-bride, then
recounted it to Mrs. Johnson, who in her dream

naughtily added stock footage of bats caught
masturbating, then told this randy little dream

to Little David, the psychic child, who got
snared in a giant spiderweb in his dream

(poor kid, stalked by rubber props of bats
and spiders, no wonder my own dreams

were so easily cursed), then told it to Willie,
who added a snarling wolf's head to his dream

(perhaps a nod to the wolf's-head cane, notorious
for smacking Willie around and, in my dreams,

for breaking my street-facing bedroom window),
then snuck into Carolyn's room to tell her his dream

(the essence of *Dark Shadows* distilled in her reply:
"You broke in my room to tell me about a dream?"),

but she escaped before he could finish talking—
not to worry, she heard the rest of Willie's dream

later, when Professor Stokes brought Willie back
to the Great House to finish recounting the dream,

part of the monocled art historian's goofy
plan to insert himself in Carolyn's dream

and break the curse—which almost worked:
Stokes appeared as the beckoner in her dream,

leading Carolyn to a foggy door that opened
onto a vision of her own gravestone (this dream

recalling Episode 224, when Maggie saw herself
lying in a casket [if you're bored by these dreams,

imagine how I felt, enduring them episode by
episode]), and she duly recounted her dream

to Stokes, who faced down the witch Angelique
on the enchanted faux-fog soundstage of his dream,

breaking the curse, it seemed (*if only!*), until nine
episodes later, when blind Sam Evans dreamed

of his daughter, Maggie, weeping at his funeral
—apparently, he can see just fine while dreaming

(maybe an effect of the dark sunglasses he wore
while comatose in his hospital bed)—the dream-

curse revived by the witch Angelique, who
then arranged for Sam to recount his dream

to Vicki, who couldn't stay awake long enough
to stall this ham-fisted plotline and dreamed

of Barnabas collapsed on the floor, dying from
a bloody neck wound, then recounted this dream

to him (the end of the line for the moronic
occult game of telephone that was the dream-

curse): Barnabas, who woke in a chair in the Old
House, seemingly unscathed by the dream-curse

(wish I could say the same for myself), convinced
that because he somehow survived his own dream

he now was cured of vampirism—only to be
bitten by a bat prop (I hoped it was a dream

within a dream, but this was too much to ask),
abruptly ending my interminable dream-curse

ghazal with two bloody neck punctures.

———————————————

Barnabas's vampire bat bite, a merciful
end (for me, anyway) to the dream-curse

plotline—"We're going to hear the dogs
howling again," Willie says on 7/15/68,

"and every night Barnabas is going to be
prowling around, and every day he's

going to be in that coffin"—but the demise
of the dream-curse wouldn't spare me,

age two, from ongoing *Dark Shadows*
nightmares, as if our TV were a magic box,

an electronic portal opened unto
the spirit world, a supernatural

transmitter documenting the undead
life of the 208-year-old creature who

lived inside the walls of my own house;
I took for granted that our TV functioned

as a conduit for a "two-directional exchange
between occultism and technology," as media

scholar Stefan Andriopoulos describes
the earliest precursors of the television:

19th-century optical devices designed
for remote viewing and clairvoyance,

leading many early 20th-century viewers to
believe that to watch TV was to experience

"the uncanny occurrence of the supernatural
or marvelous in one's own living room"—

a concept of television technology that
degenerated by 1968 into a mass-produced

rabbit-eared video receiver of a kitschy
witch-and-vampire melodrama capable

of triggering constant nightmares for
two-year-olds like myself who suffered

from insomnia even when we weren't
sleeping with our shoulders hunched

to ward off vampires (thanks to bandmate
and clairvoyant healer Allison Felus for

referring me to Andriopoulos's book,
Ghostly Apparitions: German Idealism,

the Gothic Novel, and Optical Media).

———————————

In what might be the most demented
job-interview scene in the history of

American soaps, Dr. Hoffman buries
Barnabas alive—Episode 537 director

John Weaver clearly studied at the feet of
Lela Swift, queen of the premature burial

trope—then, lingering at the fresh grave,
turns to Willie Loomis as he stutters

through another panic attack and offers
him a position at Windcliff Sanitarium,

where Willie had once been hospitalized.

———————————

"I wish I knew the secret of Barnabas
Collins," says Prof. Stokes, the show's

monocled art historian and amateur
occult detective, "he inspires so many

emotions in so many people, someday
I will understand it, I'm sure"—not so fast,

Professor, I've composed 328 sentences
for my impossible object of a poem and I'm

still confounded by crackpot story lines
like this one, unfolding now for 53 episodes

and counting: for no apparent reason,
Dr. Lang's mad-scientist experiments

somehow bestowed upon Adam a magic
power to drain Barnabas's "affliction,"

as Lang described the vampire curse,
permanently linking the fates of Lang's

Frankenstein monster and the vampire
who haunted my childhood nightmares—

"If both Barnabas and my creation live,"
Lang uttered into a reel-to-reel tape

recorder (erasing part of Mozart's Serenade
No. 13) back in Episode 486, right before

he died, "if they both live, Barnabas
will be free and healthy, as long as

Adam lives"—as if Adam and Barnabas
were the supernatural Chang and Eng

of daytime TV, sharing the same undead
body, though not physically attached

to each other (upon seeing that Chang
had died, Eng's first words were, "Then I

am going," a phrase I hope will haunt
this poem with its solemnity every time

I mock the Adam-Barnabas plotline—
Eng's words reminding me that, unlike

in *Dark Shadows*, sometimes we actually
experience the uncanny with dignity,

as when my brother turned to his wife
in their living room at the moment of

his death and said, simply, "Thank you").
July 18, 1968, two days before my mother's

42nd birthday, yet another deliriously
incomprehensible and brooding episode

introduction: "In the darkened and deserted
wing of the mansion," Vicki drones over

the show's whistling theremin, "a young
girl leads a man whose existence is the key

to a mystery of which she knows nothing"
(later, Little David returns after a 27-episode

absence, and before he can even utter a line,
the camera catches the jittery psychic child

looking offstage for his cue to speak).

———————————

Watching Episode 540 tonight with Liz,
David Trinidad, and Jeffery Conway

(visiting from Philadelphia): Nicholas
Blair, androgynous hobbit who arrived

in haunted Collinsport from Middle-earth
19 episodes ago—allegedly as the witch

Cassandra's brother—lounges devilishly
at Collinwood's tinkling pee-pee fountain:

Jeffery: "He's a gay Burt Reynolds";
Liz: "Look at Cassandra—she has *doll* eyes";

Me: "Green, Manson-girl eyes" (no one
heard me, though: I said it under my breath,

hurrying to transcribe everyone's rapid-fire
comments in my black Moleskine notebook);

David: "Look at the pink pillow: it's
totally *Peyton Place*, a '60s throw pillow—

I'm starved for those pillows."

———————————

"Congratulations, my dear, for once
you've succeeded in being successful"

—thank you, Nicholas Blair, for deriding
the witch Cassandra in the Great House

drawing room and giving me a reason
to use the word "tautology" in a poem.

Collinwood's incessant witchery makes
it easy to forget that *Dark Shadows* is still,

like all soaps, nothing but an accumulation
of endless, plodding story lines that do nothing

but enact, over and over, how ill-equipped
we all are (whether dream-cursed or not)

to navigate the rudimentary intimacies of
human relationships: Adam, such a smooth

operator for a Frankenstein monster,
learns to read poetry to seduce Carolyn,

but his awkward, nervous recitation
of Sonnet 6 from Elizabeth Barrett

Browning's *Sonnets from the Portuguese*
fails miserably (I'd hoped for an inter-

species romance between the two),
his corpse-stitched forehead sweating

in the mere proximity of her peach
minidress, then Mrs. Johnson's

ne'er-do-well son, Harry, returns
after his only prior appearance

71 episodes ago—but despite this long
absence, all his mother manages to say is,

"Have you been stealing food?"

The ignored West Wing of the Great House,
isolated and crosshatched with cobwebs—

could the writers have found a more
appropriately marginal location for Adam

to ask Carolyn what a poem means?

Watching *Dark Shadows* in my
Los Angeles hotel room the night

before I'm scheduled to read from
my book-length poem, *White Noise*,

at a CalArts writing conference:
former Shire resident Nicholas Blair

previews the social anxiety I'll feel
tomorrow, telling Stokes, no, he's really

not curious about the professor's books—
"I was just making idle conversation," he says.

That diabolical twinkle in Blair's eyes—
he's busy hatching a *Bride of Frankenstein*

scheme while Carolyn tries to persuade him
not to reveal Adam's secret whereabouts

(unlike me, Blair isn't mesmerized by
the galactic swirl of green, candy-pink,

and yellow in Carolyn's nightgown).

A dark night over Collinwood:
a stagehand coughs off camera.

A night of sudden changes on
the great estate of Collinwood:

a pocket .38 revolver in the witch
Cassandra's hands, pointed at

Barnabas ("You're too dangerous
to pity," he tells her). *A night of*

strange happenings on the great
estate of Collinwood: a dying witch

shivers between two candelabra
(nine candles total). *The long night*

of horror at Collinwood continues:
the interminable Frankenstein

plotline continues: Adam smothers
Carolyn with clumsy, wild-child kisses.

A gloomy day at the great estate of Collinwood,
a black telephone rings, phone number

COllinsport 4099—reminding me that
a half century ago, our telephone

numbers were typed on round stickers
affixed to the hub of a rotary dial

we turned with our pointer fingers
to make calls—and for one boy, sitting

in front of the television with his mother,
it's a day filled with sexual confusion:

Carolyn might be falling for a guy
created from the bodies of dead people.

On this day, a dark and terrible secret
has been revealed within the Great House

at Collinwood, a secret concerning a strange
man called Adam, who has been hiding

in the closed-off West Wing of the house:
and on this night—two hours after

I presided like a funeral director over
the release reading for the final issue

of *Court Green*, the poetry journal I
co-founded with David Trinidad

and Arielle Greenberg 12 years ago—
Adam, who already knows how to read

and has picked up scraps of grammatical
eloquence, reveals he's also discovered

one of the great secrets of soap melodrama:
when you're delivering a particularly potent

line, spin away from the camera and face
your fellow actors as if you just heard

a firecracker popping behind you.

———————————————

Eighteen candles visible in tonight's
opening scene—the Great House parlor,

Adam demanding Barnabas create
a woman for him (Adam, you're

confusing mad scientists with vampires,
Mary Shelley's amoral Victor Frankenstein

with Bram Stoker's nefarious Count
Dracula)—and I'm worried, again,

it's a bad omen the candles don't add up
to a prime number, the same baffling

affliction (explained at the end of Section 2
of this book) that makes it impossible

for me to leave my apartment without
exhausting a catalog of 39 obsessive-

compulsive checks and rechecks of doors,
faucets, electrical outlets, and oven burners,

and which now includes a 40th step that
emerged inexplicably this past month:

I'm convinced that if I don't scratch our two
cats atop their heads before I leave each day,

one of them will die while I'm gone.

"Are you putting me in the poem now,"
Liz asks, "you said you would if I watched

with you tonight": as Adam carries
unconscious Vicki to his secret hiding

place in the Great House West Wing,
he brushes against a huge soundstage

tree prop and it rocks back and forth,
nearly collapses (a clumsy *Dark Shadows*

homage to Richard Serra's brilliant
and precarious sculptures?); later,

distracted by Carolyn's sunburst orange
and green Mary Tyler Moore shift dress,

a waifish garment more appropriate
for a celebrity ashram than haunted

Collinsport, Barnabas calls her Vicki
("Vicki, aren't you the least bit concerned

that Vicki may be in danger?"), while
Adam hides the real Vicki in his closet,

which actually had been a brick wall
in previous episodes (uncomfortably

long close-up, even for a daytime soap,
of Vicki bound and gagged in the closet

—no wonder I was terrified six years
later, age eight, when the Symbionese

Liberation Army kidnapped Patty Hearst
and kept her blindfolded, gagged, tied up,

and locked in a closet for 57 days).

———————————

Despite an eight-day break from
the poem, and even with the gleeful

distraction Dr. Hoffman's awful acting
always provides ("A man—was attacked,"

she says to Barnabas, once again delivering
her lines like a nervous grad student heaving

herself through an oral exam she didn't
study for, "—and we know—how he was

attacked—and if you didn't attack him, then
—then someone else did—that means that

someone else is capable of attacking someone—
in that way—that means that—that somewhere—

somewhere in our midst, there—there is another
vampire"), I haven't been able to shake the image

of Vicki bound and gagged in Adam's closet
—not because it's creepy (it is), but because,

creepier still, it reminds me of something
I've been too embarrassed (until now)

to write about in a poem: as a child, age 4,
I was obsessed with tying up my best

friend's babysitter, a young girl probably
in high school; I didn't know the origin

of this early childhood fixation until now,
after I saw Vicki held captive in Adam's

closet in Episode 553 and wrote about
how closely I identified with Patty Hearst

in 1974, six years after Vicki's kidnapping;
tough to say whether I really wanted to be

the binder or the bound back then, considering
how often I found myself identifying with

the show's female kidnap victims—Maggie,
Carolyn, and now Vicki (22 years later, I wrote

a short story based on my oppressive office
job as a publicity coordinator for an ogre

of a boss at a jazz booking agency located
in a former funeral home in Boston's

Allston neighborhood, and I named
my first-person protagonist—a thinly

veiled version of myself—"Tania,"
after the name the SLA gave Patty

during her 57-day ordeal in the closet);
as kinks go, BDSM has never done much

for me (as an adult): a girlfriend in college
insisted on tying me to her bedposts,

but I never trusted her enough to say yes—
I was curious, of course, but I couldn't predict

what she'd do to me if I were trussed up
and helpless; deep down I felt she actually

hated me, and she was particularly
derisive, often mocking, about what

mattered most to me, once refusing to see
my band perform because, she said,

"I'm not interested in watching three
guys masturbate each other on stage";

frankly (how can I be anything but "frank"
in a vampire soap opera poem that makes

a hairpin turn into a four-year-old child's
bondage fantasy), I was afraid she would

physically hurt me, no matter how sincerely
we pledged ourselves to a safe word—

but, I must confess, all the same, as someone
raised Catholic (fled to Buddhism in my late

twenties), I was intrigued by the possibility
that pleasure might be enforced on me, inflicted

against my will as part of a performance
as intricately stylized and symbolically charged

—and erotic—as anything from our Sunday
Mass rituals of discipline and punishment

and blood and wine and mortification.

————————————

Close-up, Angelique inside her coffin
(Nicholas Blair on the verge of raising

her from the dead), vampire fangs
visible at the corners of her mouth.

I can't figure out if Blair, garishly costumed
in a silk, silver-and-black smoking jacket,

is the Devil himself or merely a comic book
supervillain: "Slaves are not supposed to ask

questions," he says to the vampire Angelique
—the show obviously continued to feed my

childhood BDSM fantasies—"nevertheless,
I shall tell you what my plan is, because

even contemplating it gives me pleasure."

————————————

Barnabas and Dr. Hoffman agree,
"the thought of a vampire is too

frightening to contemplate"—true enough,
unless, of course, you've spent the past

four years writing a poem inspired by
recurring childhood vampire nightmares

(my earliest effort to write about Barnabas
Collins dates back to my fourth-grade

creative writing class journal—an earth
brown generic notebook, the words

"Modern Composition Book" in two
clashing fonts on the front cover

and a delicious multiplication table gracing
the back, irresistible for someone like myself,

afflicted with compulsive counting
and enthralled that I could make

12 times 12 equal 144 anytime I wanted,
that I could create this numerical epiphany

just by forcing the number at the bottom
of the table's vertical axis to collide

with the number atop the horizontal—
an entry composed April 21, 1975, the day

Patty Hearst drove a getaway car
for the Symbionese Liberation Army's

robbery of the Crocker National Bank,
where SLA member Emily Harris shot

and killed bank customer Myrna Opsahl
because Opsahl didn't move quickly enough

when Harris ordered her to lie on the floor:
"One night I had the strangest nightmare,"

I wrote, "I was walking along the street
and I heard a BOOM. I looked on the side-

walk and saw two people come out of
the hole. They gave me a piece of paper.

The paper said, 'The ten most wanted
vampires.' Then I pulled a string and

the paper talked, it said, 'This paper will
self-distruct [sic] in 5 seconds.' One of

the vampires was Barnabas Collins").

———————————————

"You haven't said much of anything so far,"
Barnabas complains to Professor Stokes,

an astute summary of the 348 episodes
of *Dark Shadows* (116 hours, nearly five

full days of my life) that I've watched
since I began this poem four years ago.

I turned 49 today, wispy cool summer
breeze rustling the living-room curtains,

an unusually bland, dry afternoon for
June in Chicago—the annual deadly

heat waves that fry the pavement with
higher and higher temperatures as the arctic

ice caps melt must be coming in July
this summer—Nicholas Blair preening

in a mirror, literally twirling his dastardly
mustache like a silent-movie villain

(the vampire Angelique's reflection
mistakenly visible in the same mirror,

such a violation of conventional vampire
mythology that the writers might as well

allow her to walk brazenly in daylight),
just four days after packing my office, where

I've spent the last 12 years of my work life,
to move to a building two blocks south:

once I finished the last box—secured the lid,
stacked it alongside the 34 others filled

with books and files—the city's tornado
siren, an air-raid alert, started to blare:

a twister sighted in the western suburbs,
headed for downtown Chicago, and I felt

disembodied, waiting out the storm
in what I'll soon call my former office—

last box packed, tornado bearing down,
sky black and purple, my birthday week

begun with a funnel cloud that eventually
dissipated a half hour before it could reach

the city (I waited another 20 minutes
for my knees to stop shaking before

I boarded a Red Line train home).

———————————

Rhyming couplets, a birthday gift
For myself: Barnabas invokes Windcliff

Sanitarium, warning Willie he'll send
Him back to the madhouse unless

He agrees to begin robbing graves
For dead body parts; "We must create

A mate for Adam now," Barnabas urges
Dr. Hoffman, her sadistic mouth verging

On palsy, twitched and contorted, as she
Sifts Dr. Lang's lab notes, stifling a sneeze

While trying to understand how the mad
Scientist stitched together an artificial man

(The vampire Angelique, dimples bulging
From her undead face like a pair of bunions,

Flirts with Joe in the final scene, begging
For help to flee from Blair—then, her head

On his shoulder, she opens wide, bites his neck).

———————————

Tight close-up, Joe's black telephone
ringing: soundstage fly can't resist,

diva insect alights on rotary dial hub.

———————————

Three days before the Yippies nominate
a pig named Pigasus as their presidential

candidate at the 1968 Democratic
National Convention in Chicago,

Joe (in thrall to the vampire Angelique)
catches Willie digging up graves for

Barnabas in Eagle Hill Cemetery; poor,
panicked Willie, doomed to be Barnabas's

Pigasus—if Willie doesn't steal body parts
from the dead, Barnabas will send him back

to Windcliff Sanitarium; but if he pilfers
corpses from Eagle Hill and the police

find out, Barnabas will blame Willie's
madness, which will force the cops,

of course, to return him to Windcliff,
anyway: Barnabas's cruelty toward

Willie excites him the way blood once did,
but even though Barnabas's "affliction,"

as Dr. Lang was fond of describing
the vampire curse, has been temporarily

cured by the mere physical presence
of Adam, the show's artificial man

("If both Barnabas and my creation
live," Lang explained 75 episodes ago,

his dying words recorded on a reel-to-reel
tape machine, erasing part of Mozart's

Serenade No. 13, "if they both live,
Barnabas will be free and healthy,

as long as Adam lives"), I was too young
to understand that all you really needed

to break a two-centuries-old witch's
curse was an incoherent deus ex machina

plot MacGuffin: despite all narrative
"evidence" to the contrary, I simply

believed that Barnabas, who was so wicked,
after all, he could appear in my dreams

as one of the world's "10 most wanted
vampires" four years after *Dark Shadows*

was canceled, was still undead.

———————————

Prone in his hospital bed, two bloody
vampire puncture wounds visible

through the gauze of his neck bandage,
Collinwood handyman Tom Jennings

chokes over the word "coffin," trying
to tell Maggie he stumbled upon

a casket in Nicholas Blair's basement
in the notorious House by the Sea,

but his nurse, played by Beverly Hope
Atkinson—the first black actor to appear

on *Dark Shadows* and the only black actor
with a speaking part in the show's

1,225-episode run (nearly a full year after
today's broadcast, exactly 364 days later,

Henry Judd Baker will begin a four-
episode stint playing a character

named "Istvan, the Mute Gypsy")—
injects Jennings with a sedative before

he can spit out a coherent sentence.

———————————

Watching tonight in Madison, Wisconsin,
a month after Liz objected to the way

I portrayed her in my sentence for
Episode 553, when Adam nearly

toppled a soundstage tree prop
("I don't like that part about me:

I'm only in the poem because I *asked* to be,"
she said, adding, as I transcribed her words,

"and now you're going to keep quoting me"),
rewinding Episode 564 in our hotel room

to replay, frame by frame, director Sean
Dhu Sullivan's visual pun: close-up

of Joe, who, upon learning his cousin
Tom Jennings died from a vampire bite,

poses next to a Red Cross "Give Blood" sign
tacked to a wall at Collinsport Hospital:

exactly the kind of lighthearted goth
we needed after a miserable two-week

cancer scare triggered when an MRI
discovered an anomaly in Liz's left breast

that required a painful needle vacuum
biopsy to excavate a pathology sample

("It sounded like a dentist's drill," Liz said)
—a suspicious mass that turned out to be

a benign fibroid and atrophied tissue,
the good news coming in a late-afternoon

phone call from her doctor the day before
we left for Madison (Liz tried to reach me

after talking with the doctor, but my
train was rumbling through a Red Line

tunnel and I had no cell signal; we talked
once I emerged aboveground, the two of us

resurfacing from an underworld of imagined
surgery and chemo we could now forget—

"until my next mammogram," Liz cautioned):
the thought of losing her induced animal terror,

recalling my dead from the early 2000s
who prompted me to begin this impossible

object of a poem in the first place: my mother,
Margaret (2001), who watched *Dark Shadows*

with me every day as a child, before
I even had words to explain to myself

that I was watching television with
my mother, whose body slowly went

dark after a crippling stroke in 1999;
my brother, Carmen (2006), diagnosed

with heart disease two months before
our mother died; my ex-mother-in-law,

Virginia (2006), who died three months
after her cancer was discovered and just

one month after my brother died; my father,
Frank (2009), from cancer he survived six years

earlier that we knew would someday return;
and my cat, Shimmy (2010), who sat in the crook

of my arm and watched four seasons
of *Battlestar Galactica* with me after my

divorce, who died from heart and kidney
disease, hyperthyroidism, and diabetes,

taking a last gulp of breath wrapped
in a towel with an IV stuck in her arm

as Liz and I recited the Kaddish
and Heart Sutra: Liz, you're alive,

like Lake Mendota and the people and
their dogs at the shore, like the ducks

who trolled for food scraps tonight
and shook water from their feathery,

cottontail asses, strutting back and forth
in front of a student who watched them

watch him devour an overstuffed
bratwurst sandwich and fill his belly

with Wisconsin beer from a plastic cup
—a swarm of eating, breathing, swimming

bodies at a pier in Madison, Wisconsin,
on a night we know you don't have cancer:

Dark Shadows celebrates by staging
a bizarre variation of the soap trope

you first explained to me four years ago,
when we watched Episode 288: Barnabas

looks at the camera tonight as Willie
Loomis talks to the back of his neck,

neither of them acknowledging that
a shrouded, recently exhumed corpse

lies on the operating table between them.

———————————

Episode 565 (my next-to-last before
we move to a new apartment, across

the street from this one), listening
to the Jackie Gleason Orchestra's

version of "Love is Here to Stay"
playing on the radio in Dr. Hoffman's

Frankenstein laboratory as the shrink
trained in talk therapy tries to figure out

how to create an artificial woman
out of the body parts Willie Loomis

steals from graves of the newly dead;
later, on the DVD bonus interview,

Jonathan Frid (Barnabas) offers viewers
a theory of the vampire sublime: "Just like

Dark Shadows should have been an opera,"
he says—prompting visions of leather-lung

vocalists forgetting whole lines of song,
diva houseflies landing on black telephones

after buzzing the orchestra pit, stage props
wobbling from the force of extended trills—

"Bela Lugosi's *Dracula* should've been a ballet."

———————————

A proliferation of vampires in haunted
Collinsport tonight, fitting send-off

for the final episode I'm watching before
we move to the new apartment tomorrow:

first Barnabas, then Angelique and Tom
Jennings, and now Dr. Hoffman, who wraps

a sallow orange scarf around her neck to hide
bite marks and tells Mrs. Johnson (making

her first appearance in 14 episodes) that
she's not leaving her room—then demands

thicker draperies to keep out the sunlight;
I conceived this poem and watched its first

18 episodes—experimenting with tercets
before eventually deciding on the binary

tension of the couplet (with periodic
one-line, hanging stanzas) to convey

a childhood whose waking life only
could be understood through the fright

of its vampire nightmares (*Dark Shadows*
taught me, melodramatically, long before

Milton, that "The mind is its own place,
and in it self / Can make a Heav'n of Hell,

a Hell of Heav'n")—in a one-bedroom
apartment in Evanston, Illinois, the first

home Liz and I shared; and I've seen 299
episodes in the three-bedroom on Chicago's

Albion Avenue that we vacate tomorrow
(I wanted to write an even 300 sentences

here, but we have to unplug the television
and Bubble Wrap it tonight for the movers),

and now, preparing to leave, it's time to tally
all the cities in which I've seen at least one

of this poem's 357 (thus far) episodes:
San Francisco (7); Paris (5); Durham,

New Hampshire (4); Milwaukee (3);
Middelburg, the Netherlands (3);

Seattle (3); Madison, Wisconsin (2);
Los Angeles (2); Pittsburgh (2); Iowa City,

Iowa (2); Lawrence, Kansas (2); San Diego (1);
Chesterfield, Indiana (1); Boulder, Colorado

(1); Boston (1); Fort Wayne, Indiana (1).

———————————————

More compulsive counting, on 7/31/15,
the night before the 17th anniversary

of my move from Boston to Chicago,
after a 12-day break from the poem,

watching my first episode at our new home
(300th I've seen in Chicago): the Old House

drawing room lit by three electric candles,
Barnabas rips Hoffman's sickly scarf from

her neck, revealing two puncture wounds.
I dozed during the final three minutes

of last night's episode, hypnotized
by Barnabas's purple smoking jacket

—from his Pre-Raphaelite wardrobe
of psychedelic, shawl-collared blazers,

this one swarming with fuzzy ovoid
shapes that resembled raindrops or

amoeba or purple ladybugs—and tonight
rewound to watch the final scene again,

wide awake on 8/28/15, exactly 47 years
to the day after this episode originally aired:

Barnabas noses around like a noir detective,
hiding himself behind the pale green, pleated

double doors of Dr. Hoffman's bedroom
closet, pistol in his raised right hand

loaded with silver bullets for vampire
Tom Jennings, and director Lela Swift's

camera peeps through a voyeuristic gap
in the doors at Hoffman sitting impossibly

straight, too regal and severe, as if posing
for a drag daguerreotype: even when

the script calls for her character to remain
silent, stock-still, actress Grayson Hall

can't resist the urge to thrust her jaw
forward and twitch each shoulder

into place like a slapstick mime.

———————————————

Collinsport's resident psychiatrist preyed
Upon by vampires and humiliated by ABC's

Wardrobe department (and by Grayson
Hall's overacting): Hoffman staggers, knees

Buckling, through the Great House doors
Hunched and gasping for breath, as if she just

Surfaced from a scuba accident ("Of course,
She's been practicing that entrance for months,"

Liz says; we've stopped trying to make sense
Of Hall's 1964 nomination for Best Supporting

Actress in *The Night of the Iguana*), her dress
an ungainly mess of garish plaid, sporting

A sad-clown bow-tie collar from shoulder
To shoulder with a blue silk scarf hastily tied

Around her neck; later, the end-credit scroll
Inspires me to steal the show's closing tagline,

"Fashions courtesy of Ohrbach's," for line seventeen
Of this mock-heroic sonnet to a boy afraid of sleep,

Barnabas plotting to bite him in a dream.

———————————

Queen of the premature burial trope,
director Lela Swift was more dangerous

to children than the vampires, witches,
warlocks, and Frankenstein monster

that haunted Collinsport (only 90 episodes
until the show's first werewolf appears);

cursed by Angelique, Mrs. Stoddard
believes she'll be sent back to Windcliff

Sanitarium, where, she's convinced,
the doctors are conspiring to bury her

alive, further proof for a two-year-old boy
watching with his mother in Pennsylvania

on 8/30/68—in front of the TV whose
Sesame Street broadcasts taught him

how to read that same year—that if adults
couldn't protect themselves from the terrors

of premature burial, then he should expect
to wake up one night, shoulders hunched,

trapped underground in a casket.

———————————

Dr. Hoffman's "Self-Portrait in a Flat
Hand Mirror," her right hand smaller

than her head thrust at the camera, and her
left hand swerving easily away, as though

to protect what it advertises: a golden
candelabra on a marble desktop, a French

reading chair, old beams, Hoffman's bare
neck—whose two bite marks disappeared

after Barnabas staked Tom Jennings through
the heart (looking down at the helpless

vampire asleep in his coffin, as if seeing
himself distorted in a convex mirror,

Barnabas said to Jennings, "Did someone
ever look at me as I look at you now"—

director Sean Dhu Sullivan's gloomy,
sepulchral camera shot of Jennings

in the casket was Barnabas's reflection
once removed); Hoffman's face swims

toward and away in jittery, overacted
repose—sequestered in the glass—

puckering but inanimate, like an Ashbery
sentence blurred beyond recognition by

its own meandering, oracular declarations.

—————————

I'm Jack Spicer listening for radio
signals from beyond, prepared

to take dictation from his Martian
muses—watching for a *Dark Shadows*

epiphany, an occult manifestation
to mark the end of this book, but

tonight's episode (viewed twice)
reveals nothing but irritable bickering

and disassociation—Joe admits he's not
reasonable, Maggie is tired of arguing

and being stood up, and Dr. Hoffman
lapses into a fugue state at the bottom

of the Old House stairs. Dawn comes
to Collinsport, heralded by harp and

theremin and Nicholas Blair rapping
at the door of Sam Evans's studio,

where Joe and Maggie sit, chaste,
an agitated black-and-green afghan

draped across the back of Sam's sofa—
the same afghan that covered Jeremiah

and Josette's bewitched marriage bed
back in 1795 at the Collinsport Inn

("Get me the pills, Maggie," Joe says).

Credits

(1795-96)

Barnabas Collins..Jonathan Frid
Naomi Collins...Joan Bennett
Joshua Collins..Louis Edmonds
Abigail Collins...Clarice Blackburn
Daniel Collins..David Henesy
Jeremiah Collins..Anthony George
Jeremiah Collins's ghost...Tim Gordon
Voice of Jeremiah Collins's ghost............................Addison Powell
Millicent Collins..Nancy Barrett
Josette du Prés...Kathryn Leigh Scott
André du Prés..David Ford
Countess Natalie du Prés..Grayson Hall
Angelique Bouchard...Lara Parker
Victoria Winters...Alexandra Moltke
Reverend Trask...Jerry Lacy
Ben Stokes...Thayer David
Peter Bradford..Roger Davis
Navy Lt. Nathan Forbes...Joel Crothers
Suki Welles Forbes ("Sookie") ....Jane Draper
Noah Gifford ("Danny Bonaduce look-alike")................Craig Slocum
Reverend Bland..Paul Kirk Giles
Maude Browning ("Maudie")..Vala Clifton
Maude Browning's ghost..Maggie Benson
Phyllis Wick..Dorrie Kavanaugh
Bathia Mapes ("Angel of Death")..Anita Bolster

(1967-68)

Barnabas Collins..Jonathan Frid
Elizabeth Stoddard Collins (Mrs. Stoddard)......................Joan Bennett
Roger Collins...Louis Edmonds
Carolyn Collins Stoddard..Nancy Barrett
David Collins ("Little David, the psychic child")...........David Henesy
Sarah Collins ("Ghost Girl")...Sharon Smyth
Cassandra (Blair) Collins...Lara Parker
Nicholas Blair..Humbert Allen Astredo
Victoria (Vicki) Winters...Alexandra Moltke
Maggie Evans..Kathryn Leigh Scott
Sam Evans...David Ford
Joe Haskell..Joel Crothers

Willie Loomis..John Karlen
Dr. Hoffman..Grayson Hall
Dr. Lang...Addison Powell
Dr. Woodard...Robert Gerringer, Peter Turgeon
Tony Peterson ("Lawyer Peterson")...Jerry Lacy
Professor Stokes...Thayer David
Jeff Clark...Roger Davis
Adam...Duane Morris, Robert Rodan
Mrs. Johnson...Clarice Blackburn
Harry Johnson..Craig Slocum
Tom Jennings..Don Briscoe
Nurse...Beverly Hope Atkinson
Sheriff Patterson..Vince O'Brien
Burke Devlin.....................................Mitch Ryan, Anthony George
Jason McGuire...Dennis Patrick

Tony Trigilio's most recent books include Book I of *The Complete* Dark Shadows *(of My Childhood)* (BlazeVOX [books]), *White Noise* (Apostrophe Books), and *Historic Diary* (BlazeVOX [books]). He is also the editor of *Elise Cowen: Poems and Fragments* (Ahsahta Press) and author of the critical monograph *Allen Ginsberg's Buddhist Poetics* (Southern Illinois University Press). He hosts the poetry podcast Radio Free Albion and plays in the band Pet Theories. He is a member of the core poetry faculty at Columbia College Chicago, where he is Interim Chair of the Department of Creative Writing.

Made in the USA
Middletown, DE
16 October 2016